D0287853

STATE AND NATION

POLITICS

Editor

PROFESSOR W. A. ROBSON,
B.SC. (ECON.), PH.D., LL.M.

Professor Emeritus of Public Administration in the University of London

Other studies on the subject by the same author

Der Rechtsbegriff der Minderheit
(Zeitschrift für öffentliches Recht, 1929)

La sociologie de la nationalité
(in *La Nationalité*, Sirey, Paris, 1933)

Le droit des minorités
(in *La Nationalité*, Sirey, Paris, 1933)

Jews among the Nations
(American University Digest Press, Washington, D.C., 1936)

Pan-Arab Nationalism
(*Asia*, 1939)

The Jewish Question after the War
(*Harpers*, 1941)

Nationalism Today and Tomorrow
(*Tomorrow*, 1944)

Israel and the World
(*American Perspective*, 1949)

Politische Probleme Poly-Ethnischer Gemeinwesen
(Politische Vierteljahresschrift, 1962)

forthcoming

Political Problems of Poly-Ethnic States
(Proceedings of the Round Table of the International Political Science Association, ed. B. Akzin, Atherton Press, New York)

STATE AND NATION

BENJAMIN AKZIN

Herbert Samuel Professor of Political Science
and Constitutional Law at
the Hebrew University of Jerusalem

HUTCHINSON UNIVERSITY LIBRARY
LONDON

HUTCHINSON & CO. (*Publishers*) LTD
178–202 Great Portland Street, London, W.1

London Melbourne Sydney
Auckland Bombay Toronto
Johannesburg New York

★

First published 1964

This book has been set in Times New Roman type face. It has been printed in Great Britain by The Anchor Press, Ltd., in Tiptree, Essex, on Smooth Wove paper.

Contents

I

The terminological jungle

THE purpose of the present volume is to enquire into the relations existing between two major social phenomena—the political phenomenon of the State and the ethnic phenomenon of the nation. The issue is joined whenever the two meet in the arena of human affairs, and this happens often enough in the course of history, indeed more often as we approach our own day and age. The encounters assume special importance when they relate, as they usually do, to politics. In this field the State is an acknowledged major factor. The role of the nation in politics, on the other hand, is controversial. The very legitimacy of the injection of the nationhood concept and all its derivatives into the world of politics is still a matter for debate. Protagonists of nationalism regard it, and the nation behind it, as a deservedly decisive factor in political history. Opponents consider it a factor at once dangerous and extraneous, brought somewhat artificially into a picture where it had no business to be in the first place.

The subject-matter is inevitably complicated by the fact that neither term is uniformly understood in either theory or practice. 'State', with a capital S, is a term used to denote anything from the United Kingdom to the Sultanate of Sarawak, from the United States of America to the State of Nevada, from the Union of the Soviet Socialist Republics to the Republic of Carelia, from the Swiss Confederation to the canton of Basel-Stadt, from France to Monaco, from Italy to San Marino, from Spain to Andorra. Nova Scotia, Rio Grande del Sul, Queensland, Styria and Bremen are all States in the broad sense of the word, variations in the official nomenclatures notwithstanding. The use of the term becomes more uncertain yet when we reach back into the past, with hundreds of 'States', ranging from large to miniature, cluttering up the map of Europe from the Renaissance (when the term was first coined) onward, and perhaps still more so if we try to apply modern terminology to feudal Europe, to Mediterranean antiquity or to the autochthonous political formations of pre-colonial Asia, America and Africa.

For the jurist and the legally oriented political scientist the essential point in this terminological issue is whether to confine the use of the term to those political bodies which successfully claim the attribute of sovereignty, i.e. legal independence from any other human organization—*societates quae superiorem non recognoscunt*, in the language of Jean Bodin—or whether to extend this use to those entities as well which claim and exercise no more than limited autonomy; and in the latter case —how far downward should such use be extended? To the historically minded political scientist, to the sociologist and to most non-specialists the term *State* connotes, somewhat vaguely, a political formation of sufficient stability, sufficient resources and sufficient power to make its writ respected over a reasonable period of time and space by inhabitants and foreign 'States' alike.[1] Without attempting to decide the issue for all purposes we shall best suit the purpose of the present study if we lean towards a fairly broad use of the term at the risk of including in our field of vision some marginal entities whose claim to statehood is open to challenge because of insufficient authority or power. Where States are to be observed in order to examine their relations with the ethnic phenomenon of nationhood it seems better to err on the side of liberality than to risk overlooking significant developments because of too narrow a definition.

Still greater difficulties are presented by the term 'nation'. In the English language, *nation*, as well as its derivatives, such as

1. Modern sociologists and anthropologists often refuse to acknowledge as States societies characterized by a pre-technological stage of development, clan-based or tribal structure, and a system of norms dominated by magical concepts. The correctness and usefulness of this attitude are open to doubt, but the point is of no relevance in our context.

national, nationality, nationalism, nationalization, are used to denote concepts intimately linked to the State at least as much as phenomena connected with ethnic groups, if not more so. We speak commonly of a British, an American, a French, a Spanish nation, when what we have in mind is the circle of persons bound to Britain, the United States, France or Spain by bounds of 'allegiance' as determined by the laws of these countries—a circle which coincides fairly closely, though not completely, with the sum total of these countries' permanent inhabitants. Similarly, a 'national', as commonly used in the English language, is a citizen or subject (though in some countries the terms are distinguished by legal shadings) of a given State; 'nationality' is the quality of citizenship or subjection to a State, imputed to an individual; the adjective 'national', as in 'national interest', is an attribute assumed to be that of the State and its population taken as a whole; 'nationalization' is the turning over of ownership to State authorities. And so is 'nationalism' used occasionally with reference to strong attachment whose objects are a State and its alleged interests. A similar meaning is given to the equivalents of these terms in French and in other Romance languages. An outstanding example, ever since Rousseau, is the French expression *souveraineté nationale,* which means the attribution of sovereignty to the whole of the State's population, while in the English usage *national sovereignty* indicates that the State as such is sovereign without naming the actual bearer of sovereignty within the State; neither expression has anything to do with the so-called 'nationality principle', the postulate according to which a nationality (in the ethnic sense) has a claim to be organized as an independent State.

And yet all these terms, with the single exception of 'nationalization', are used simultaneously in English and in Romance languages, overwhelmingly in German and in the Slavic languages, in the sense of an ethnic group or a relationship based on it. This is particularly true of the very modern and very controversial term of 'nationalism'. The basic difference between the usages is not, as in the case of the term 'State', a difference of degree or shade; it is rather a difference of essential meaning. In order to introduce a minimum of clarity in our treatment, a choice between these wholly different essential meanings must be made and adhered to. Without, therefore, denying the legitimacy of other uses of our terms in different contexts, the meaning we shall attach to the terms in question throughout this volume will be that of a certain type of an *ethnic* group[1] and of relations based thereon.[2] Indeed, only if this meaning is attributed to our terms does the subject of our enquiry make any sense at all: for in its other meaning, where *nation* tends to coincide with the demographic element in statehood, our problem would resolve itself into a near-tautology and would amount to nothing else but an enquiry into the relation between the State and the sum total of human beings who form the State. What we are concerned with, however, is neither a terminological debate nor a semantic refinement, but the very real complex of conflicts, of attempts at compromise and harmonization, and of mutual influences of two forces, the one political, the other ethnic, when they meet with mankind as their common ground, actors and object.

Of the two basic concepts, statehood, for all the imprecisions involved in it, is the one more generally understood. Nationhood, in our sense, is the relatively unknown factor. Further elucidation of nationhood and its principal concomitants will therefore have to be undertaken before we proceed to the examination of the main patterns of the State-nation relationship.

1. Precisely what constitutes an *ethnic* group is not much clearer than what constitutes a *nation*. The usefulness of the term *ethnic* lies in its being more neutral and freer from emotional overtones of approval and disapproval than the term *nation* and its derivatives.

2. The only concession that will be made to the other meaning will be in the use of the term 'international', which when spelled in this manner will be given the usual meaning of 'inter-State'. When denoting relations between nations the word will be spelled 'inter-national'.

2

Attitudes and literature

THE literature on both statehood and nationhood is abundant indeed. States and statehood constitute the central topic of history and political science and occupy a prominent place in jurisprudence and other branches of the law, in philosophy, sociology, cultural anthropology and theology, among other disciplines, not to mention folklore, poetry and fictional prose. The phenomenon has been examined from all possible aspects, in relation to its internal functioning as well as to external factors, as material for objective observation and description, and as object of value-judgements by partisans and detractors alike. This literature is too broad in scope and too varied in character to be mentioned here; those interested will find it under the respective appropriate headings. Some of the sources take up the relation between State and nation, and the more significant of these will be named occasionally in the following pages.

One recurrent feature of the literature on the State should be retained at this point because of its importance in our context: on the whole, statehood as a form of social organization characterized by a highly effective and legitimized monopoly of the use of physical force in human society on a large scale has fared remarkably well at the hands of its observers and commentators. Opposition has been expressed quite often by thinkers, teachers and writers, as well as by the man-in-the-street, to this or that regime, to this or that policy, to this or that State, even to the idea of a particular as distinct from a universal State; but statehood as such has emerged unscathed and was approved by well-nigh all. The basic explanations for this attitude, and the basic justification of statehood as a desirable system of social organization, have been provided, as far as Western civilization is concerned, by Plato in one form, by Hobbes in another. Even monotheistic religious thought, averse to statehood on principle, saw itself compelled to make its peace with it, as is indicated by the Pentateuch and the Book of Samuel, by Jesus's and St Paul's injunctions to render unto State authorities that which is due to them, by St Ambrose, St Augustine and Pope Gelasius, by Muhammad, by Luther and Calvin.

Only two significant and related currents of thought started with denying the value of statehood in general: one was the so-called utopian socialism, branching off in anarchism and syndicalism; the other was Marxian socialism. However, the first of the two currents, beginning with wholesale disapproval of organized force for the sake of voluntarism, has ended its career by substituting, both in theory and in practice, disorganized violence for organized compulsion, thereby losing much of its persuasive power. As for Marxian socialism, it took its stand on the affirmation that the State as such may and should wither away once a desirable social order will have been established, but in fact, both in its social-democratic and in its communist versions, it made the State its foremost instrument. True, Marxian socialists of both persuasions have stressed that the use they made of the State was temporary only, just as utopian socialists stressed the merely transient use they made of violence. But once more the pragmatic French observation according to which, in politics, *ce n'est que le provisoire qui dure*, seems to have justified itself, and the Stateless future of Marxian philosophy takes on increasingly the appearance of an eschatological vision indulged in the more fervently just because it stands in so blatant a contrast to an ineluctable and unattractive reality.

This positive value which is generally bestowed on the idea of statehood, however much opposition its specific forms and manifestations may encounter, is important in our context. The two phenomena of State and nation do not always meet as harmonizing and complementary forces; quite often they constitute competing forces. The value placed on them by onlookers is one of the factors which determine their respective influence. The fact that the State represents a principle of social organization which, by dint of long practice and universal familiarity, is taken for granted as a legitimate force by most observers lends it a considerable advantage. The further fact that the literature too overwhelmingly approves of the State gives it an added advantage and should be taken in consideration when dealing with the treatment accorded to our topic in the sources. Not only actual States, with their powerful enforcement machinery, but also most scholarly and literary sources, with all the intellectual and emotional stimuli conveyed by them, are facing the nation when it assumes the character of a dynamic force and, under the name of nationalism, tries to enter the sphere of politics.

The literature concerning nationality, though very prolific too, can by no means bear comparison with that directly devoted to the State or indirectly conveying the message of statehood, and is of comparatively recent vintage. Until the nineteenth century nationality was, relatively speaking, a side-issue on the intellectual horizon of European civilization, nourished though the latter was on the intense nation-consciousness of the ancient Jews and Greeks as revealed in the Old Testament and in Greek sources. Those few who pondered over the phenomenon prior to that time realized from the beginning that nationality was very relevant to political organization and therefore to statehood, and treated it accordingly.[1] Two writers of the thirteenth century—both of them

1. Among the fullest recent studies of the early literature on the subject, as well as on the early evolution of nations and nationalism, one should name: C. J. H. Hayes, *The Historical Evolution of Modern Nationalism*, 1931; F. Hertz, *Nationality in History and Politics*, 1944; H. Kohn, *The Idea of Nationalism*, 1944. Dealing with the same subject, but somewhat lacking in clarity, is: E. Lemberg, *Geschichte des Nationalismus in Europa*, 1950. Several interesting essays on the subject are assembled in: H. Koht *et al.*, *La Nationalité et l'histoire*, 1929; and a further stimulating essay is J. Bowle's *The Nationalist Idea*, 1955. An excellent brief study of the emergence of early nations, as being themselves products of the integration of several ethnic and racial groups, is the Smithsonian Institute pamphlet of J. R. Swanton, *The Evolution of Nations*

Englishmen, as it happens—Roger Bacon and Bartholomew, known as Anglicus, were among the first to call attention to the nation as factor in State and society. On the verge of the fourteenth century Dante unites an underlying respect for the ethnic group as the basic unit of political organization with a deep longing for peace and order on a larger scale. His solution is therefore a multi-national Empire in which the national States would be no more than autonomous formations. With him, therefore, opens the long succession of thinkers who combine an understanding for the national aspirations of the individual nation with an over-all international outlook. Substantially the same line is followed by John of Paris and by Marsilius of Padua, except that they laid more emphasis on the national State and less on the inter-national superstructure and that the Church rather than the Empire appeared to them as the appropriate vehicle for the desired compromise. One should remember, of course, that with all three of them and with most writers of the following century the ethnic basis of statehood was but a weakly traced side-issue; their principal interest centred on the issue of secular versus temporal power.

Step by step the national factor in politics draws upon itself the attention of European scholars, partly as an object of dispassionate study, partly as a factor to be either deplored or welcomed and furthered. This is quite understandable in the light of the growing importance which the national idea has assumed in fact: it has played a significant part in the strengthening of the 'national kingdoms' at the expense of Empire, Papacy, feudal lords and 'foreign' foes; in the Reformation; in the revolution of the Netherlands; in the growth and political unification of Russia. But then, like all other ideas, the national idea, too, owes a great deal to those writers and thinkers who have developed and spread it.

1942. Swanton studies the phenomenon itself, not the literature on it, and the end of his essay is marred by tendentious conclusions. The best over-all bibliographical guide on the subject of nations and nationalism, up to the time of its publication, is: K. S. Pinson, *A Bibliographical Introduction to Nationalism*, 1935. A later bibliography, almost as comprehensive for the period covered, is: K. W. Deutsch, *An Interdisciplinary Bibliography on Nationalism, 1935–1953*, 1956.

By the eighteenth century, though the principal interest of the intellectual leaders of the time was still occupied by other problems, chiefly the problems of individual liberty and of man's search for cognizable truths, the literary treatment of the national factor grows more prominent. Again it is an Englishman, Lord Bolingbroke, who is the first to pay much attention to the claims of nationalities in politics, and he does so in an approving vein. He is followed in England by David Hume, Edmund Burke and Jeremy Bentham. In France Montesquieu observed the phenomenon rather dispassionately, but Jean Jacques Rousseau did come out as an advocate of the national factor in politics. It is noteworthy that the authors named here belong otherwise to quite different schools of thought.[1] The main centre of a vast nation-oriented literature, both on an intellectual and on an emotional level, is found, however, in Germany. Johann Gottfried von Herder serves as its most prominent fore-runner, and under the impact of the French Revolution and the Napoleonic wars it assumes the role of the dominant intellectual fashion in the beginning of the nineteenth century. It now indeed is allied with a romantic interpretation of history. The opposition, however, is by no means negligible. Opposition to a nation-oriented view is centred on the one hand in the proponents of a God-given dynastically motivated State *à la* Bossuet, and on the other hand in that outlook which considers the individual and mankind at large as the supreme values—an outlook which sometimes veers more towards the rational, at other times towards the humanistic, which can be traced back to the Epicureans and Stoics of old, and whose foremost spokesmen during the period under discussion are Voltaire, Goethe and Kant.

The nineteenth and, thus far, the twentieth centuries are those periods in history where the national factor, aided by the dynamic political ideology based on national attachment and known as nationalism, has shown itself most powerful. This is

1. It is therefore a mistake to describe nationalism, as some authors are prone to do, as wholly an outgrowth of romanticism, Bolingbroke, Hume and Bentham would hardly fit into this picture.

the period in which national movements in Europe have, for better or for worse, wrought deep changes in the political map of the continent, resulting in the wholesale shifting of boundaries, in the mutilation of pre-existing States, in the creation of new ones and in considerable modifications in the internal policy and structure of quite a number among them. Naturally enough, this process has been mirrored in the literature of the period. On the whole, we find the literary treatment in Germany, Italy, and at a somewhat later time in Eastern Europe and the Near East, favourable to the national factor in politics, while in Britain, France and the United States the attitude of observers and commentators is rather sceptical and occasionally hostile.

There are good and valid reasons for this difference. In the first-named group of countries State and nation covered two glaringly divergent groups of human beings, and while the cause of the nation gained in attraction by being essentially voluntaristic, preaching self-determination and rule by consent of the governed, and therefore allying itself with the fashionable principle of democracy, the State machinery sought legitimation in no-longer-fashionable authoritarian principles, suffered from insufficient identification with ethnic values and to a sizeable proportion of its subjects seemed based on brute force only. Of the second group of countries, Britain and France represented a far greater measure of convergence between State citizenry and the national group, and the State structure itself was far more consistent with democratic theory. The latter was also true of the United States, but in addition that country, for reasons which will be explained later, lacked national groups intent on pulling their full weight in politics. On the contrary, emphasis on the ethnic group might have torn asunder that country of mass-immigration. A special case was that of Switzerland, too small to affect the main currents of political thought, but presenting a peculiar interest and a lesson all of its own: here, indeed, several ethnic groups co-existed in a single political structure, but that structure, through the cantonal system, had made peace long ago both with the rudiments of democracy and with the heterogeneous composition of its population, thereby reducing considerably the trend towards either general radicalism or dynamic nationalism. Leaving aside the Swiss case, which began to attract major attention at a later time, it is not to be wondered at that the educated élite took its stand largely with the advocates of nationality in the first group of countries, with those of the State in the second group.

The intimate connection between the scholarly and literary treatment of the issue and the political background and interests involved will appear still more clearly if we take a closer look at the position assumed by various participants. In Belgium we shall find a different tone prevalent among Flemish than among Walloon observers. In the great Irish controversy most English writers took a stand fundamentally different from that of most Irish commentators. Even in the first group of countries we find the political claims of the nation advanced mostly by writers belonging to non-dominant nationalities in poly-ethnic States or to nationalities splintered politically between several States; the claims of the State—by writers belonging to the dominant nationalities of poly-ethnic States.

It is especially interesting to pursue this development in England. Here we witness a curious reversal of the earlier position. Among the major figures of nineteenth-century England only three men stand out as having fully understood and largely advocated the political claims of nationality. They were the supremely nonconformist Byron, John Stuart Mill—whose nonconformism in this regard was paralleled by and to a certain extent logically connected with his other political nonconformism, *viz.* his advocacy of proportional representation—and Disraeli—whose Jewish descent will have made him sensitive to the viewpoint of a non-dominant nationality.[1] Far

1. Characteristically, Disraeli's acceptance of nationality as a major factor in politics is most clearly expressed in his fiction and historiosophic reflections. In his political activity Disraeli subordinated his attitude towards nationality to what he considered to be the pragmatic interests of England and the Empire. Our understanding of Disraeli's position should not be influenced by the fact that he, like many others of his and of succeeding generations, used words such as 'nation' and 'race' in several meanings. It is only after gauging the exact meaning attached to the term

more typical of the attitude of nineteenth-century England towards the State-nation problem are the views expressed by men like Carlyle, Coleridge, and especially Lord Acton, the final passages of whose essay on *Nationality*, vehement in their rejection of its claim to a major political role, continue to exercise influence to this day.[1]

It would be interesting to speculate on the causes of this reversal. A plausible explanation might lie in the fact that in the eighteenth century Scottish, Welsh and Irish heterogeneities, and the political institutions connected therewith, were still generally accepted. In the nineteenth century integration had progressed in the United Kingdom, and the interests of the Realm, both with reference to the British Isles and with reference to the Colonies, required an underemphasizing of nationality claims. When Irish resistance became too strong to overcome it was thought better to treat Ireland as a special case than to elevate it to the position of an example for a universally valid principle. However that may be, even the leading nonconformists of the late Victorian and Edwardian eras—Shaw, Wells, the Webbs—viewed the nationality principle rather doubtfully. Their intellectual radicalism and Fabian socialism expressed itself within the political framework of man—State—and possibly class; but they disliked the idea of nationality as a fourth reference point. Only where movements of national emancipation could be equated with demands for individual advancement or social progress did they meet with the whole-hearted approval of that school. Significantly enough, greater insight into the political claims of nationality is shown at the beginning of the present century by a group of men whose intense preoccupation with international politics made them realize its strength: Joseph Chamberlain, Balfour, Lloyd George, Lord Cecil of Chelwood, Milner, Smuts and—in

in a given context that we are fairly entitled to reach conclusions as to the author's attitude. This should be borne in mind in connection with the occasional misinterpretation of Disraeli's sayings concerning England's 'two nations' or the all-important role of race.

1. An outstanding example of this influence is Elie Kedourie's *Nationalism*, written for the present series and first published in 1960.

the United States—Woodrow Wilson. But just because this group was composed of active politicians their views on the problem were always subject to adjustment in the light of pragmatic political considerations. The basic indifference and occasional hostility of English thought at the height of the British Empire to the national idea can, indeed, be likened to the circumstances under which the leading minds of ancient Rome found in a mixed Stoic-Epicurean philosophy—also a philosophy that minimized the ethnic moment—a trend of thought most congenial to the task of empire. And though English opinion and policy, from Canning through Palmerston to Gladstone, frequently gave their support to national movements, this, in so far as it was due to ideology or sentiment and not to purely political considerations, was based on the desire to assist libertarian movements against absolutism or to help in the liberation of Christian peoples in the Balkans from Moslem rule rather than on the acknowledgement of a general principle of the right of nationalities to statehood. Only in 1918 and briefly thereafter, when, partly under the influence of a Russian revolutionary slogan and partly as justification for the desired break-up of the Austro-Hungarian and Ottoman empires, the principle of self-determination was made part of the declared aims of the policy of the Allied Powers, did the national idea enjoy a period of relative favour in the English-speaking world.

Nineteenth-century France was integrated ethnically at least as much as contemporaneous Britain, was less preoccupied with questions arising out of rule over a hetero-ethnic colonial empire, and was far more intensely engaged in designing a satisfactory pattern of State institutions. Consequently, French literature and scholarship of the period yield little that would tend to strengthen the claims of nationality in politics. This was so despite the fact that French intellectuals, wide awake to contemporary events, could not fail to notice the struggle of national movements, chiefly of Italians, French-speaking Walloons, Hungarians and Poles, against the States in which they were incorporated, and tended to sympathize with them. A deeper and more positive interest in the national problem arose in France only after the Franco-Prussian War of 1870 and can be traced to the emergence of Alsace-Lorraine as a French national *irredenta.* The main exponent of this development was Ernest Renan, whose lecture *Qu'est ce qu'une nation*, delivered in 1882, remains one of the classical expositions of the problem. Nevertheless, the ethnic phenomenon of the nation remained marginal in French life and thought, and the State was never dislodged from its central position as the unchallenged framework of political organization. The principal development of the theory of nationalities occurs in Germany of the 1806–48 period, with Fichte and Schlegel as its main exponents, and somewhat later in Italy, under the spiritual guidance of Mazzini, spreading from there to the non-dominant nationalities of Austria-Hungary and the western fringes of Russia. The Balkan nationalities, without worrying much about theory, were in practice among its earliest beneficiaries.

Particular mention should be made of the attitude or, rather, attitudes, adopted by socialist theoreticians of various shadings towards the incursion of the national idea in politics. The views of British Fabian socialists have already been noted. Pre-Marxian socialism was interested in political organization as an instrument for either a desirable or an undesirable socio-economic order, not as an instrument for expressing or developing ethnic characteristics. Indeed, attachment to the latter was regarded by early socialist authors as a pointless prejudice. This, essentially, was also the view of Marx and Engels. As a matter of principle, they and most of their disciples took a negative view of the national idea in politics, both because they regarded it as part of an anti-proletarian ideological superstructure erected by the exploiting classes, and because it threatened to substitute unity of classes within a nation for the desired unity of the proletariat across national boundaries. In practice a more pragmatic standard of judgement was used: specific nationality claims tended to be judged by most socialist thinkers and politicians depending on the manner in which they were likely to affect progress towards a socialist society. Where certain nations were to be encouraged in their political struggle (e.g. Poles against the Russian Empire, Italians against Austria) this was because they were regarded as more progressive than the State that held them in subjection. It was as actual or potential forces of progress rather than because of any inherent claim of nations to statehood that they were entitled to support. This view was essentially followed by German social-democrats led by Karl Kautsky, and by the British Labour Party.

A more positive view towards the place of nationality in politics was taken by social-democrats in countries with acute ethnic tensions, presumably in an effort to identify themselves more fully with the political strivings of underprivileged ethnic groups, and by social-democratic groupings among non-dominant nationalities to whom the handicaps under which their ethnic group was placed were a keenly felt experience. Leadership in this development was assumed by the social-democrats of Austria, Belgium and Russia—three countries in which ethnic national tensions rose to considerable height at the beginning of the century. Outstanding among them were the Austrian social-democratic leaders Karl Renner and Otto Bauer. Renner's *Staat und Nation*, 1899, and *Der Kampf der österreichischen Nationen um den Staat*, 1902 (published under the pen-name Rudolf Springer), and Bauer's *Die Nationalitätenfrage und die Sozialdemokratie*, 1906, gave detailed expression to a viewpoint which acknowledged national self-determination as a generally valid principle, but sought to satisfy national claims, wherever possible, on the basis of federalism, of territorial or of personal autonomy, stopping short of the demand for absolute independence. A great deal of sympathy for the national idea was shown also by the social-democrats of Italy, themselves emotionally involved in the recent national movement of *risorgimento*, as well as by those of France and the Netherlands, under the warm-hearted leadership of Jean Jaurès and Camille Huysmans.[1] With all

1. No valid generalization may be made in this respect about the attitude of Jewish socialists. While specifically Jewish socialist groups, chiefly the *Bund* in Eastern Europe in the early part of the century and the Zionist socialist parties, shared in the credo of national self-determination and advocated more particularly its application to the Jewish community according to their various views, Jewish socialists can be found on all sides

these groups, 'national self-determination' began to lose the character of an opportunistic slogan or of a convenient aid to progress, and became a constituent feature of a triple credo, along with socialism and political democracy. The future withering away of national differences, foreshadowed by early socialists, was either pushed into an eschatological future along with the withering away of the State, or gave way to simple internationalism—the demand for a non-aggressive, co-operative co-existence of nations.

Communist views on the national question mark a measure of return to Marx. More acutely alive to tactical considerations than most social-democrats, Lenin and Stalin[1] clearly perceived the importance and usefulness of advocating a dignified political status for the subject ethnic groups in Russia and in the colonial areas of the world. Far, however, from ascribing to the existence of individual nations a permanent or intrinsic value in itself, they frankly stated their hope and belief that these will gradually give way to coalescence. In practice, uncompromising nationalism is still preached to the masses (though not to the communist-indoctrinated élite) in those regions which are considered as undergoing struggle with Western imperialism. In the Soviet Union and the other multi-national countries within the communist orbit, on the other hand, the cultivation of ethnic characteristics and the maintenance of national autonomy of non-dominant nationalities are practised wherever advisable, but intrinsic attachment to separate national iden-

of the issue, from the total denial of the validity of the national idea, to its general acceptance in respect of nations but excluding the Jewish community from their definition of nation, and to the communist view later to be explained.

1. Lenin's views on the question are found throughout his writings, but especially in his essay *The National Question* (see the English edition of his *Selected Works*, n.d., vol. IV, pp. 250–293). Where Stalin was concerned this issue was the first and only major doctrinal issue to which he had devoted his attention before entering the period of personal power; it was also the focus of his first major post in the Soviet Government, as Commissar for the Affairs of Nationalities under Lenin. His volume of essays and speeches, *Marxism and the National Question* (also translated into English), which, as distinct from his later writings, undoubtedly represents his own work, is a major contribution to the subject.

tities is already down-graded as 'bourgeois nationalism' and ultimate integration is praised as more consistent with true socialism. It should be added that this attitude is shared by theoreticians of the Yugoslav brand of communism as well. In observing this trend one may not overlook the added strength which increased national integration lends to the dominant nationality and to the State in which a given nation predominates. The point has certainly not been lost on political leaders in communist-oriented countries, and the preaching of the virtues of integration, cautiously directed at the secondary nationalities in communist countries, is not unconnected with the increasingly nationalist and patriotic overtones lately adopted by leading spokesmen in the Soviet Union, in China, in Poland, in Rumania and in other communist-dominated countries. Thus, in the East, no less than in the West, it is seen that minimizing the claims of secondary nationalities is quite consistent with the affirmation by spokesmen for a dominant nationality of the value attached to their own nationality's continued existence and to its political pre-eminence in the given State.

Another significant trend in the literature of the last century is that which strongly affirms the superiority of the author's own (or favourite) nationality over all others, or at least over some others. Awareness of one's belonging to a given nationality and a purposeful self-identification with it (the so-called national consciousness) are intensified in this trend to the point of transforming the alleged superiority, and the other nations' alleged inferiority, into a major belief which is used to justify the application of radically different standards to their respective needs or claims. This double-standard treatment of national claims is no longer a feature of political opportunism born out of mildly ethno-centric preoccupations such as characterize any group of human beings. It becomes a basic ideology, under which the most trivial needs or interests attributed to one nationality take precedence over the most pressing needs or interests of others, and fear of effective sanction serves as the only brake on the nationalist's aspirations. Whatever the psychological or psycho-pathological explanations of the phenomenon, its result is that the theory of nationalities as a universally valid theory applicable in principle to all nationalities is openly discarded, and nationalism is preached as a particularistic doctrine, valid with reference to one's favourite nationality, but of questionable validity or completely irrelevant where other nationalities are concerned. Xenophobia, instead of being an instinctive reaction to a lack of wide-ranging social communication or an incidental by-product of special tensions, is elevated to the status of a virtue. The trend thus characterized is responsible for some of the worst barbarities in history, with those committed during the Nazi regime most gigantic in scale and fresh in everybody's memory.

Quite often in history this strongly particularistic and aggressive version of nationalistic doctrine was able to develop on the usual basis of the national group as characterized by one of the more common combinations of ethnic characteristics. In recent decades we find a similar development in the literature of Italian fascism and of near-fascist movements in other countries of Latin civilization. But in other cases the usual nation-producing mixture of language, culture, physical proximity, common political organization and a varying measure of common descent does not seem to suffice in order to produce the mental and emotional climate here described. A stronger and more tangible basis is required, and this need is fulfilled by the emphasis placed on the vaguely physical concept of *race* as the principal criterion of nationality. Quite common in primitive and oriental societies where real or presumed descent from common stock is the accepted *rationale* of ethnic differentiation, and never quite extinct, the racialist approach has experienced a doctrinal revival in the nineteenth and twentieth centuries, with Joseph Arthur de Gobineau's *Essai sur l'inégalité des races humaines*, Houston Stewart Chamberlain's *Grundlagen des neunzehnten Jahrhunderts* and Alfred Rosenberg's *Mythos des zwanzigsten Jahrhunderts* as its principal expositions. The 'white race' as a whole, and the Nordic, Indo-Germanic or Aryan 'race' more especially, was and still is the main object of solicitude for the authors belonging to this school, and its teachings form the theoretical mainstay of the German Nazi movement as well as of fascist and near-fascist movements in all countries in which one of the Germanic languages prevails. The 'coloured races' and, within the 'white race', the Jews are most frequently cast in the contrasting role of 'inferior race', with all consequences flowing therefrom. However, other 'races'—Arab, Chinese, Japanese, Jewish, Magyar, Slavic, among others—are also occasionally represented in this light of a particularly noble or superior group whose racial purity or political claims are entitled therefore to particular consideration. Of late, symptoms have appeared, both in Africa and among the Negro population of the United States, of the Negro 'race' being similarly glorified.

Political history since the First World War has brought in its wake three major developments directly relevant to our problem. In the first place national movements have stepped over the boundaries of Europe and have become an explosive force all over Africa and Asia; indeed, aided by a favourable international constellation of inter-Power and inter-bloc rivalry, nationalism has become the principal ideological concomitant of the de-colonization process. In the second place the destructive and barbaric potentialities inherent in the national idea, in its aggressive version here described and already foretold by earlier imaginative minds,[1] were terrifyingly illustrated by the excesses perpetrated in its name in Hungary, fascist Italy, Poland, more recently in Algeria, Angola, Kenya and other areas undergoing de-colonization, and on a particularly horrible scale in Nazi Germany. In the third place, in Europe itself, the cradle of modern nationalism, second thoughts begin to prevail on the subject after the Second World War, leading to its down-grading on the scale of social values and subordinating the slogan of national independence to that of international co-operation or even to inter-State and inter-national political coalescence. Having played with sovereignty and

1. An amazingly prophetic description of these potentialities, with special reference to German nationalism, will be found near the end of the third book of Heinrich Heine's *Geschichte der Religion und Philosophie*.

having abused it for centuries, the States of Europe begin to get tired of the toy; and Europe's nations, those human groups which either enjoyed or sought to enjoy the game as its real beneficiaries, grow disillusioned about the blessings of that extreme formulation of the principle of nationalities which sees its optimal expression in sovereign independence.

As a result of these developments, we find today, beside the older and still amply represented schools of decided protagonists and just as decided antagonists of nationality in general or of a specific nationality in particular,[1] a more sophisticated approach which is less Europe-centred, less dogmatic about the values involved and less preoccupied with approving or disapproving a given set of solutions. Instead, this group of scholars is mainly engaged in observing and analysing the national factor in society, in tracing the sociological and psychological roots of the phenomenon, in gauging its strength and effects, in examining its spread into new areas and the possibly new forms it may assume there and in scrutinizing the manner in which various solutions of the problem have worked out in practice.

Among the early writings of this new and objective trend in the literature on the national question one may name works such as A. Zimmern's *Nationality and Government*, 1918; W. Pillsbury's *Psychology of Nationality and Internationalism*, 1919; V. Lovett's *History of the Indian Nationalist Movement*, 1921; A. van Gennep's never completed *Traité comparatif des nationalités*, 1922; Sir E. Barker's *National Character and the Factors in its Formation*, 2nd ed., 1928; H. Kohn's *History of Nationalism in the East*, 1929, followed by his other writings; the studies, already mentioned, by C. J. H. Hayes; and the

1. The 'anti-national' trend in the Actonian tradition has received a special fillip from recent developments in Europe and is therefore particularly active today. Its most outspoken representatives are E. Kedourie, *Nationalism*, 1960, and W. Sulzbach, *National Consciousness*, 1943, articles in *Politische Vierteljahresschrift*, vol. 3, 1962, and *Zeitschrift für die gesamte Staatswissenschaft*, vol. 118, 1962. The attitude is also shared, with modifications, by F. Hertz, *Nationality in History and Politics*, 1944, and—from the Catholic angle—by L. Sturzo, *Nationalism and Internationalism*, 1946.

report on *Nationalism* by a Study Group of the Royal Institute of International Affairs, 1939.

Further research in this vein has been abundant since the Second World War. Leaving aside material published in form of review articles and naming only some of the outstanding monographs, one should mention A. Cobban's *National Self-Determination*, 1945; F. Znaniecki's *Modern Nationalities*, 1952; K. W. Deutsch's *Nationalism and Social Communication*, 1953; L. L. Snyder's *The Meaning of Nationalism*, 1954; T. Hodgkin's *Nationalism in Colonial Africa*, 1956; R. Emerson's *From Empire to Nation*, 1960, and the earlier *Government and Nationalism in South-east Asia*, published in 1942 by the same author in collaboration with others; J. Plamenatz's *On Alien Rule and Self-Government*, 1960; J. M. Ahmed's *Intellectual Origins of Egyptian Nationalism*, 1960; W. H. Wriggins's *Ceylon: Dilemma of a New Nation*, 1960; T. Kerekes's *Arab Middle East and Muslim Africa*, 1961; I. Wallerstein's *Africa: The Politics of Independence*, 1961; Jean Buchmann's *Le problème des structures politiques en Afrique noire indépendante*, 1961, and his *L'Afrique noire indépendante*, 1962.

The same search for objective analysis, removed as far as possible from partisanship, can be observed in a series of newer works devoted more particularly to the especially delicate problem of national minorities. Thus: C. A. Macartney, *National States and National Minorities*, 1934; O. Janowsky, *Nationalism and National Minorities*, 1945; J. A. Laponce, *The Protection of Minorities*, 1960. Of special importance is the brief but excellent memorandum on *Definition and Classification of Minorities*, submitted by the Secretary-General of the United Nations in 1950 (U.N. Document E/CN.4/Sub.2/28, 27.12.1949). The memorandum contains not only a very serviceable analysis of the term 'nation' and a highly useful political classification of national minorities, but also a very good bibliography on the whole subject of minorities up to the time of publication. Prior to the 1930s the best bibliographical source on the subject was J. Robinson's *Das Minoritätenproblem und seine Literatur*, 1928.

Of late, the international community of scholars has also

started coming to grips with our problem in a series of co-ordinated studies. Major examples of this kind of endeavour are the papers collected in the volumes of I.N.C.I.D.I. (Institut International des Civilisations Différentes) as well as the papers presented at the Round Tables organized by the International Political Science Association in 1961 and 1962 and by the Association Française de Science Politique in 1962, soon to be published.

3

The phenomenon of the nation

THE point of departure for our study is the ethnic group at the point when it begins to loom either as an active factor in an existing political structure or as a challenge to such a structure. It is at this point that one begins referring to the ethnic group as a nation or nationality in the widest use of the term.[1] A brief look, however, should be taken at the ethnic group as such, irrelevant of its political significance.

Like all social categories the ethnic group is an approximate characterization or description of a given segment of humanity marked by a trend prevalent within it. It does not imply that the characteristics involved must inevitably be present in every single individual or in precisely ascertainable doses. For this reason social categories in general and ethnic groups in particular do not lend themselves to precise definitions. This holds true of nations, in the ethnical sense, as well.[2] We shall there-

1. It will not be attempted, in this book, to ascribe any distinct specific meanings to the words *nation* and *nationality*. Quite often, however, are politically conscious ethnic groups referred to as nationalities as long as they have *not* become dominant in an independent State, and as nations once they have achieved this status.

2. Several authors who have dealt with our topic have dwelt at length on the difficulty or impossibility of a precise definition of a nation in the ethnic sense and have tended to conclude that the very concept of a nation in this sense is a useless or an unreal one. See e.g. W. Sulzbach, 'Zur Definition und Psychologie von "Nation" und Nationalbewusstsein' (*Politische Vierteljahresschrift*, vol. 3, 1962, pp. 139–58). We believe this view to be methodologically erroneous and to spring from a desire to demonstrate as non-existing a phenomenon which the author in question regards as undesirable. It is true, of course, that a nation in the politico-legal sense, being a normative construction, lends itself far more easily to precise definition. This does not exclude the possibility that ethnic

fore have to describe, rather than to define, the ethnic group.

The term springs from the Greek *ethnos*, which has been variously translated for modern usage as *people*, as *nation* or —by substituting a human group for the more or less cohesive environment in which it lives—even as *country*. Neither of these expressions is capable of precise definition any more than the ethnic group, and for exactly the same reason, but this does not invalidate them as possibly useful characterizations of existing social categories. The adjectival form *ethnic*, as used today, indicates those characteristics, whatever they may be, which, being prevalent within the group and distinguishing it from other groups, lead us to consider it a people apart. A people is the man-in-the-street's equivalent of what the scholar calls an ethnic group. The meaning conveyed by both terms is that of a group most members of which are relatively similar in certain respects to one another, while being dissimilar in these respects from most members of other groups. This 'similarity-dissimilarity' pattern is constituted by what we call ethnic characteristics.

The relative importance of these characteristics varies from period to period, from case to case and from school of thought to school of thought. Those most frequently named are a common language and a common tradition of *mores* and culture. A degree of common descent, without being vital, facilitates the development of these features and is often found to exist, especially in the case of older ethnic groups formed in relative isolation. A further characteristic, of utmost significance in the more distant past, but of rapidly diminishing importance as we approach modern times, is a common religion; still, in a number of cases it continues to be influential as basis for 'peoplehood' and its concomitant claims. Thus Catholicism in relation to Ireland, Islam in relation to Pakistan and Judaism in relation to Israel. Another example is that of the Polish national movement in the nineteenth and early twentieth centuries, where the Catholic religion of most Poles,

nationality may become the subject of legal regulation, as was indeed the case in many a pluralist regime, and therefore capable of being precisely defined.

contrasting with the predominance of Protestantism among Prussians and of Greek Orthodoxy among Russians, helped to cement the Polish ethnic community.

Thus far, only *objective* criteria of a non-political nature have been mentioned. *Subjective* criteria, i.e. those consciously cultivated for the sake of their group-cementing effect, and the influence of political structures on ethnic groups, will be taken up later on. Basically irrelevant to the existence of ethnic groups, though of immense social importance in themselves, are those characteristics which are primarily related to social stratification, to uniformity or otherwise of economic levels and occupations, to diversity of cultural levels within the same culture, and to prevalent or competing secular ideologies. Relative uniformity in any of these respects, if it occurs in an ethnic group, obviously broadens the basis of its homogeneity and intensifies its cohesiveness. Diversities in any of these respects, just as obviously, detract from the group's homogeneity and cohesiveness, without, however, destroying that minimum of cohesion which permits us to view it as an ethnic group.

The point at which the ethnic group enters our special field of interest is that at which it has both exceeded purely local dimensions and become of significance in the political sphere. It is at that point that the appellation of nation or nationality can be applied to it. Size is an important aspect of the phenomenon. As a matter of principle, any group of people characterized by the similarity-dissimilarity pattern noted above might have been regarded as a nation, whatever its numbers and geographical distribution. In this sense a village community in the tropics, based on kinship and sufficiently isolated from other village communities in the same general area to have but scanty communication with them and to develop a distinct dialect, could be called that. But in current language we tend to confine the use of the term to a group that extends in numbers far beyond a single kinship community and in expanse far beyond a single locality. Therefore, where no sufficient communication has developed within a given region to result in a pattern of considerable cultural similarity, we say that the people of that region have not yet coalesced into a nation, and that they live in a kinship stage, a tribal stage, a parochial (to use anachronistically an expression borrowed from an entirely different context) stage, but at any rate in a pre-nation stage of society. This implies that the national group is not coeval with mankind, but presupposes a fairly advanced civilization with ample communication between smaller social units within the area. A number of civilizations of the ancient world—those of China, India, Persia, Mesopotamia, Judaea, Egypt, Greece, as well as a number of advanced civilizations of pre-Columbian America—can undoubtedly be regarded as having reached the stage of nationhood. Some pre-modern civilizations—those of Celtic, Germanic, Semitic, Slavic and Turanic origin—and of some pre-colonial societies in Africa—might be regarded as having been well on their way to nationality formation. But other, primitive and near-primitive, societies could be said to have remained at the pre-nation stage of development down to our age.

The second feature which is taken for granted in a group regarded as a nation or nationality is that of major significance in a political context. The term did not acquire this meaning at once. In classical, post-classical and medieval Latin *natio* was only one of several terms used approximately in the sense of the Greek *ethnos*, and by no means the most widespread among them; *gens*, more particularly, was a serious competitor. It is well known that *nationes* in medieval times was used most often without any political connotation. It is only towards the end of the Middle Ages that *natio*, both in Latin and in newer European languages, outstrips its rivals, gains wider circulation and acquires a political meaning. It obtains a kind of official recognition in the context of the 'Holy Roman Empire of the German Nation'. This political connotation of the term, once established, has never been lost. Indeed, we saw that quite often, and especially in English and in Romance languages, the connotation becomes so dominant that it tends to dislodge entirely the original, ethnic, meaning—a usage which should well be noted, though it will not be shared in this study.

It follows from the above that our interest in an ethnic group tends to diminish as and when its political influence is reduced, as and when it loses its character of a *national* group. Thus the ethnic groups known as Macedonians or Croats or White Russians, as distinct from other Southern Slavs or from Great Russians, have exercised and continue to some extent to exercise through their distinctiveness a noticeable effect on the political structure of the society in which they live. On the other hand, Bretons and Provençals and Savoyards and Plattdeutsche and Calabrese and West Virginia mountaineers and Pennsylvania Amish, though no less distinguishable from their French and German and Italian and American neighbours, have had their distinctiveness reduced to the cultural sphere only, to a variety in *mores*, even to a kind of colourful folkloristic oddity, but without any special claim or effect on politics. Basques in Spain, Scotsmen and Welshmen in Britain, can be said to lie somewhere in the middle between the two groups of cases, with their future development uncertain, but with odds favouring their evolution towards the non-political kind of ethnic group. Using the term in the widest practicable meaning, we shall speak of a national group when an ethnic group exercises in fact or effectually strives to exercise major influence on the political structure of society.[1] Such influence can be the function, as it were, of the mere numerical and cultural weight of the given group, and without any deliberate organized effort to that effect; it can also result from a conscious effort to maintain or to shape a political structure in which the values of the ethnic group would find the utmost satisfaction possible under the circumstances. In the first place

1. We may disregard in this connection that rather trivial form of political influence which is expressed in a mere successful attempt to have members of the group well represented among elected or appointed holders of public office. This feature, leading at times to careful 'balancing' of public offices between various ethnic groups, is encountered often enough in poly-ethnic countries and taken by itself does not warrant the conclusion that we are in the presence of well-crystallized national groups. If, however, the feature endures for a long time, and is increasingly accompanied by additional claims for political recognition, it is a symptom to be carefully watched.

we deal with a nation which historically, before the advent of the era of nationalism, has become organized as a State or has at least achieved recognition for political purposes in part of it. In the second place we deal with a nation which has achieved this position or is striving towards it under the impulse of nationalism.

It is in vain that we shall search in the nature or in the extent of objective similarities and dissimilarities for a clue to the riddle why some ethnic groups have become, or are showing signs of developing into, nationalities, while others have not crystallized into nations or have ceased to appear as such. The cases mentioned before demonstrate this fact. The first group of cases, drawn from the Slavic world, are not 'objectively' more dissimilar from their neighbours than the second group selected from Western Europe and the United States. All over Latin America far-reaching distinctions in language, culture, *mores*, standards of civilization, religion, even in racial make-up, colour and general physical appearance, have failed to develop—at least up to the present—that typical pressure for a formal political recognition of the ethnic group which would justify us in considering it a nationality even in the embryonic stage. A similar situation obtains in the case of many a well-pronounced ethnic group in the new poly-ethnic States of southern Asia and of Africa. On the other hand, phenomena such as the tension between Singhalese and Tamils in Ceylon, the drive of certain ethnic groups in India for recognition as autonomous States within the federation, the position of the Shan tribes in Burma, the federalization of Congo and Nigeria on an ethnic basis, do indicate that we are in the presence of an emerging poly-nationality pattern. Generally speaking, where ethnic groups exist side by side, one may not be certain when pressure for their adequate political recognition will make itself felt. The extent of their objective dissimilarities will not be the decisive factor in making for this development or in hindering it, and certainly exhortations by scholars who frown on nationality will have no major effect. Other factors, into which we shall enquire later, will prove more relevant. For the moment it will suffice to retain that the line between an ethnically based nationality which becomes an active factor in politics and an ethnic group that does not amount to a nationality is both uncertain and shifting.

The exaggerations so often indulged in on either side where the subject of nationalism is discussed force us to bring back the issue to its proper proportions at the risk of stating the obvious. Let it be emphasized, then, that even where nationalities have fully crystallized and, due to circumstances, the purposeful dynamic trend known as nationalism has gained wide adherence, these are far from constituting the only major force that manifests itself in history. Society is essentially pluralist, in that the individual finds himself bound in a manifold fashion and to several overlapping groups. The average adult in a developed society is at once member of a household, of an inner family, of a wider family or kinship group, of a circle of habitual friends, of a wider circle of casual acquaintances, of a neighbourhood group, of a group related by a similar educational level, of one or several groups with whom he has shared a common experience (school alumni at different levels, fellow-veterans, fellow-employees, even fellow-vacationers or tourists), of an occupational group, of a group with identical economic interests, of one with a similar level of economic well-being (the three being by no means identical), of a group of worshippers at the same shrine, a wider group of communicants of a single religious denomination and a still wider circle of adherents to a single group of denominations linked by a common basis (e.g. Christianity or Islam or Judaism or—still wider—monotheism), of a linguistic group, of a regional group, of one or several (in a federation) political structures, of a nation, and of any number of ideological or way-of-life or hobby groups (e.g. conservative, socialist, pacifist, vegetarian, nudist, lover of classical or jazz music, stamp-collector, hunter, etc.). Each one of these links produces objective effects of similarity and diversity as well as subjective attitudes of solidarity and alienation; none of them, perhaps, more than the socio-economic links which result in the long run from an extreme difference in economic well-being—an effect which Disraeli had in mind in his often-quoted and often-misquoted utterance about the 'two nations' of which England was composed. But no human being is characterized by membership in one group only. Each one has links with several of them, and no two groups have an identical membership. To some extent this reduces, at times even completely neutralizes, the effect of any one of them. And the nation is no exception.

The list of social links here given is far from being complete. In many a case one should add to it links such as partnership in business or in a co-operative, membership in a political party and other associations pursuing material or non-material interests. Here again, while the ensuing circles may attain a fairly high degree of convergence, they are never completely convergent, and thus the pluralist character of man's loyalties is never quite lost.

It has been noted already that nations as such are not stable phenomena, but rather shift about on the stage of history, some disappearing, others making an appearance. This constant shifting is still more characteristic of the membership in any given nation. It is not only through the passage of generations that this membership changes. Even the nationality status of a single individual is subject to change, affected as it is by migration, intermarriage, gradual alienation from one national group and gradual integration within another. Nationality in the ethnic sense, unlike citizenship, cannot be changed by a specific official act, but neither is it immutable. The intensity of an individual's identification with it is subject to change; the act of identification itself is subject to change; the objective finding that an individual belongs to a given national group—in so far as such a finding can be made on the basis of objective criteria—is subject to change; and marginal cases abound in the shape of persons whose national links have been seriously upset—the so-called uprooted or de-nationalized persons—without having gained sufficient objective identity and subjective identification with a new nationality.

In underdeveloped and more traditional societies the number of group-links is much smaller and their stability is much greater, but then in societies of this kind the very phenomenon of the nation is less crystallized, thus again reducing its weight within the complex of forces which influence society.

The preceding remarks will preserve the reader from falling into the error of a 'monistic' view of society. Placing a special value on some link or idea in preference to other links or ideas is not a rare occurrence among men. But going to extremes in this direction is typical only of fanatics. We find it among fanatic nationalists no less, but also no more, than among fanatic patriots, religionists, liberals ('give me liberty or give me death!'), socialists, racialists, pacifists, caste-conscious brahmins or aristocrats. Therein lies the social dynamism which all such views, links, ideas and attitudes exhibit occasionally, their power to influence society far beyond their quantitative dimension within the sum total of the social forces. If we look at it objectively, however, no single link or idea constitutes more than one among many influences in the life of even its most fanatical adherent, let alone in the lives of the total membership of any given group. Basically, the pluralism of any given society, be it even a monastic order, remains unimpaired.

This determines the place of the nation in society. Not present everywhere and at all times, not acting upon every single individual and certainly not acting upon every individual affected with equal force, it nevertheless represents a very real, very widely held, often very influential, form of a social link, one that has exercised and continues to exercise powerful influence upon society. It is a question of a different order, whether the influence it exercises is, on the whole, a desirable or an undesirable one. Opinions on that may differ. It may be well to refrain from too generalized an answer.

4
Mono-ethnic and poly-ethnic States

THE simplest model of a nation is that of a politically organized ethnic group—whether sedentary or nomadic—living in relative isolation from other ethnic groups, a phenomenon quite frequent in technically underdeveloped societies until the very recent past. The political organization formed by such a group will be, accordingly, a mono-ethnic State.[1] In such a structure the lines of the political and of the ethnic community will tend to coincide, both objectively and in the subjective consciousness of the members of the community. Just as in primitive societies the lines between the State-given law, the precepts of religion or magic, the norms of morality and those of custom tend to be blurred, and these systems tend to flow together, so, only probably to an increased extent, will the lines between State and nation be hard to distinguish in a mono-ethnic State.

What has just been said will help us to understand the reasons for the previously mentioned insufficient awareness in

1. As previously remarked, we may disregard for our purposes the somewhat arbitrary distinction drawn by several modern anthropologists between a political and a kinship society. Where a network of social institutions succeeds in effectively regulating relations within a human group, gains acceptance as an arbiter free to legitimize or to refuse legitimacy to activities within the group, and does so with the aid of actual or potential use of organized compulsion, we can say that a political organization has come into being. Thus: S. N. Eisenstadt, 'Primitive Political Systems', in: *American Anthropologist*, vol. 61 (1959), pp. 200 ff. That the institutions thus functioning are based on actual or alleged kinship relations is irrelevant. If the system thus described is 'independent' of extraneous political rule, or if its 'dependence' on an extraneous system is merely occasional, it will certainly constitute a State; and here again a kinship basis won't alter the situation.

Britain and France of the phenomenon of ethnic nationality and for the consequent use of the term in the two languages to denote the whole of a State's permanent population. Britain and France neither are nor were in the past mono-ethnic in the strict sense of the word, and they certainly don't live in isolation from other States and nations. But in both cases convergence between the two circles of the total State population and of the total membership of the predominant ethnic group is sufficiently close to leave most observers in these countries with the impression that the two are, broadly speaking, identical. Hence the use of terms 'nation' and 'nationality' in both senses; hence, because the State is a far more concrete and easy-to-grasp concept than the ethnic group, the prevalent use of the terms in a State-centred meaning; and hence the bewilderment and occasional annoyance of British and French observers—close students of foreign affairs apart—when the seemingly simple and harmonious situation is beclouded by the intrusion of an extraneous ethnic concept which threatens to bring a discordant note into 'the unity of the nation' and incidentally is used to justify the claims of the State's outlying and hetero-ethnic possessions to independent status.

In a purely mono-ethnic State the problem of State-nation relations simply doesn't exist, for the two entities do not stand in juxtaposition to each other, and a clash between them is unthinkable. A sophisticated foreign observer, were he allowed to study it, might be able to differentiate between the two concepts, saying—along with Herder—that the State in question was an organized expression of the *Volksgeist* or—to use more contemporary language—that the State's institutions conform to the *mores* and other characteristics of the given ethnic group. For men and women inside the mono-ethnic State there would be no distinction between the concepts: the State's population and the ethnic group, the official language and the language of the people, would be identical, and there the matter would rest. If, in addition, we deal with a fairly primitive, undifferentiated, State machinery, they would similarly identify the established State religion with the religion of the people, the law of the State with the rules of custom, with traditional family-patterns and food-habits and dress-habits and social manners that have evolved in a non-organized fashion within the ethnic group.

It is a plausible assumption that such mono-ethnic States did exist, both before written history began in a given region and in the historic past. European explorers of other continents and islands have recorded the existence of such States in recent centuries down to our times. Anthropologists have given us further evidence of such native States. And even some States admitted to be part of the modern inter-State community (significantly called 'family of nations')—Saudi Arabia, Yemen, Tibet, Nepal, Bhutan—have only recently begun to emerge from this stage. There is no need to assume, in dealing with mono-ethnic States of the kind here described, that they have been such from the very beginning. It is quite possible that the populations involved are themselves the product of an integration process of several ethnic components, a process that may have occurred either before the formation of the State observed or at some subsequent period. What matters is that by the time we observe the State, this process has been completed and the very memory of it has more or less vanished from the consciousness of the people.

The decisive turning-point from our point of view is reached when a State ceases to be purely mono-ethnic. This can happen in a multitude of ways. Let us sketch out some of the simplest:

(a) A small fairly isolated State comes into warlike contact, whether by land or by maritime raids, with a society whose population differs ethnically from that of our State. A number of prisoners are taken on the battlefield and are brought back. If they are permitted to stay alive in whatever status, possibly as slaves or in another subordinate capacity, the State and its population are faced with the fact that there exist in their midst persons with 'foreign' ethnic characteristics who none the less form part of the political community.

(b) A small mono-ethnic State, as a result of warlike contacts, conquers and subjects to its rule a village or a group of villages which hitherto lay outside its territory and which is inhabited by people of a differing ethnic make-up. Again, the demographic composition of the State is no longer mono-ethnic. Conquerors and conquered alike are faced with the question whether and on what terms to adjust to this new reality.

(c) As a result of peaceful contacts, mostly commercial, 'foreigners' plying their trade or other occupation begin to appear in a hitherto mono-ethnic State, and some of these take up there more or less permanent residence. Again, a hetero-ethnic element has entered on to the scene, and neither State authorities nor the population at large may assume any longer that membership in the ethnic and in the political community is necessarily identical.[1]

(d) Over a period of time, aided perhaps by population growth or by territorial expansion, significant differences develop in the *mores*, language or religion of a population formerly homogeneous in these respects. Where religion is concerned it may be a case of a sudden reform movement or the rise of a new inspirational or magic religion, or dissension on a point of ritual or dogma; outside of the religious field the change is apt to be slower and more gradual. Whatever the circumstances, the State's population, at the end of the process, may no longer be ethnically homogeneous.

In all situations previously mentioned the assumed identity between the political and the ethnic community is shaken by

1. A possible way out of the difficulties is the granting of what is known in legal parlance as a distinct 'personal status' to persons of differing ethnic characteristics or antecedents. They are regarded accordingly as belonging to a different 'nationality', as 'aliens'. The ethnically foreign persons become thus regularized as foreign to the political community as well, even though they intermingle with the rest of it geographically and to a considerable extent socially as well. This pattern was especially developed in medieval Europe and should be regarded as fore-runner of more modern forms of ethnic pluralism. However, history has shown that the attempt to keep an ethnically foreign group politically distinct is difficult to maintain in the long run unless it is bolstered by strong-arm methods of segregation and discrimination.

the appearance of hetero-ethnic elements within the State. A different type of non-identity confronts us in the case of an ethnic group which, for whatever reasons, finds itself divided between a number of States, while occasional contacts with other ethnic groups foster among its members by contrast an awareness of their common ethnic characteristics. The case is the familiar one of the Anglo-Saxon inhabitants of early England; of the French before the unification of France in a single kingdom; of the Moors in Spain; of Christian Spaniards before their political unification; of Russians during the period of the principalities; of Italians and Germans till well into the nineteenth and partly even into the twentieth century; of Poles from the end of the eighteenth century till the First World War. Sufficient contact was maintained by the groups concerned with both their kin across political boundaries and with compatriots of differing ethnic make-up to produce a high degree of awareness of ethnic homogeneity and heterogeneity, with ensuing tensions and claims. Strictly speaking, cases of this kind do not quite belong in the present context, for some of the States concerned (e.g. individual German and Italian States before their respective unification under Bismarck and Cavour; Austria after 1918) may well be fairly mono-ethnic. But the non-congruence between the State and the ethnic community is illustrated just as vividly by a State which fails to embrace the total ethnic group as by the State which embraces several ethnic groups or parts thereof; and the results of this kind of non-congruence are apt to be, in certain circumstances, just as explosive.

Under modern conditions the purely mono-ethnic State has become an anachronism, and an almost vanished one at that. The transposition of frontiers following the meanderings of political history on the one hand, and the increased mobility of mankind due to the development of commerce and communications on the other, have transformed practically every State on the face of the globe into a poly-ethnic one. There are, however, States in which the dominant ethnic group is so well integrated and occupies so overwhelming a position in respect of numbers and status, and in which the secondary ethnic groups are relatively so insignificant, that the latter may be ignored for most practical purposes. States of this kind—Sweden, Norway, Denmark, the Netherlands, post-war Poland, Hungary, Bulgaria and Greece, to name the best known among them, and to a smaller degree France and Britain—face the problems of poly-ethnicity to a minor extent only, as a largely transitional issue pending the full integration of any existing hetero-ethnic groups. Only exceptionally, under the impact of internal socio-economic crises, of external factors, and of strongly exclusivist, exaggeratedly 'nationalistic' ideologies, can tension due to poly-ethnicity rise even in such States to the point where it may cause grave difficulties and suffering. In the absence of these special conditions such States' restricted poly-ethnicity results in but trivial problems and may be fairly disregarded under the maxim of *de minimis non curat praetor.* From the point of view of the casual observer there is little to distinguish these States from mono-ethnic ones.

In other States, however, poly-ethnicity is a central rather than a lateral issue. Such a case may be due to the yet incomplete ethnic integration of the main mass of the inhabitants, to the larger numerical proportion of non-dominant ethnic groups in relation to the total population, to a strong concentration of a non-dominant ethnic group in part of the State's territory and especially in a border area, to discrepancies between the numerical weight of the different groups and the cultural or economic status held by them, or to other circumstances connected with geography, politics or ideology and apt to exacerbate incipient ethnic tensions. The problems posed by poly-ethnicity in such cases are of a durable character, and their solution in one manner or another may seriously affect the structure and social climate of the State involved, in extreme cases even its territorial integrity or its very existence.

In this type of poly-ethnic States the issue becomes particularly acute if one or more of the ethnic groups within them have been aroused to present claims of a political nature bearing on the basic values or organizational structure of the State concerned and must therefore be regarded as *nationalities.* The initiative of this attitude may be seized either by the dominant ethnic group—a nationality by any standards—or by one or more of the non-dominant groups. The appearance of a non-dominant ethnic group in the role of an active nationality beside the dominant one transforms the State into one which is not merely poly-ethnic but also multi-national. The struggle between the principal antagonists comes now into the open. On the one hand there is the articulate leadership of the dominant nationality, which is also the spokesman for the State and has the main instrumentalities of the State machinery at its disposal. This leadership struggles at one and the same time for the integrity of the State and for the maintenance and strengthening of the position of that nationality in it. At times this aim is pursued by way of furthering the ethnic *integration* or assimilation of the non-dominant nationalities into the dominant one, a trend which is anyhow facilitated by the long-term effects of physical proximity and of the pressure of the larger mass on smaller groups. At other times the effort to maintain the State's integrity is coupled with an attempt to keep the line between the nationalities clearly demarcated, reserving the dominant role in the State to one of them and relegating the others to a subordinate position. In this latter case the pattern aimed at is not one of integration but of *pluralism* (i.e. durable co-existence of several groups and their respective cultures within the same State) *on the basis of inequality*. To the extent that the integrationist pattern prevails, it is the attachment to the State—*patriotism*, to give it its commonly used name—that is pushed into the foreground, while the attachment to the dominant nationality—*nationalism*—though present, occupies a less conspicuous position in the background. Where the pattern of unequal pluralism shows up it is the dominant nationality's nationalism that occupies the centre of the stage while the State is valued mainly because of its role as an instrument in the service of the nation.

On the other side of the fence we find the secondary or non-dominant nationalities in the State. Their articulate spokesmen, unless they are willing to relinquish their claims and characteristics as a distinct nationality, are moved by the potent ideology already encountered, named nationalism. But in this case the object of the national or nationalist[1] movement, rather than to protect the existing political *status quo*, is to change it in the interest of the given nationality. The forces of the *status quo* entrenched in the State machinery and allied with the leaders of the dominant nationality will confront then the advocates of the secondary nationalities pressing for change. Each force will seek to subdue the antagonist or, failing that, to achieve the best possible compromise.

1. The attempt is often made to distinguish between 'national', 'national-minded', 'national liberation movement' and similar expressions, to be used in an approving, and 'nationalist' or 'nationalistic' in a disapproving, sense. See, e.g., L. Sturzo, *Nationalism and Internationalism*, 1946, pp. 4 ff., 27 ff. While appreciating the motives behind this distinction, we don't believe it feasible to maintain it.

5

Nationalism

THE existence of ethnic groups, the members of which exhibit sufficient similarity and coherence among themselves and sufficient differences from members of other groups to warrant objective recognition as such, is a well-nigh universal fact of history since its beginnings and even antedates written history. Nations or nationalities in the sense employed in this study, i.e. more-than-local ethnic groups whose characteristics and *mores* decisively influence political structures, constitute an almost equally ancient and wide-spread phenomenon. On the other hand, the *consciousness* of belonging to a nation, coupled with an active urge to perpetuate and strengthen national bonds by various, including political, means, is relatively new and less than ubiquitous. It was the exception rather than the rule, a state of mind found among ruling or educated élites rather than a mass movement, until the beginning of the nineteenth century in Europe and even until a later time in the rest of the world. It is this state of mind which has since developed into a powerful ideology, vaguely described as *national-mindedness* or *nationalism.*

When saying this we should by no means overlook the instances of the appearance of nationalism in earlier times among large groups of populations. Without going beyond the familiar breeding-grounds of Western civilization, we shall recall once more those strong indications of nationalism among ancient Jews and Greeks, already mentioned before. Further indications of it are found in Persia, Carthage and early Rome. For centuries Hellenistic and Roman civilizations, the Roman and Byzantine empires, Christianity and later Islam, exercised a strong integrating and assimilating influence; ethnic distinctions became blurred in many cases, and still more blurred became, under the impact of other-than-ethnic values, the attachment to the ethnic group and the urge to regard it as a factor deserving of a pre-eminent part in shaping politics. Nationalism, therefore, declined, without disappearing altogether.

By the ninth century nationalism begins to show signs of a revival and starts leaving its marks anew in historical records. In the Moslem East there emerge symptoms of what may properly be considered a Persian, an Arab and later a Turkish national consciousness which is expressed not only in cultural but also in political terms. In the Christian West the division of Charlemagne's empire shows the influence, among others, of the ethnic factor, and despite the intrusion of rival feudal and dynastic concepts, this ethnic factor never again disappeared from the European scene. On the contrary, it grew gradually stronger and contributed in a large measure to the transformation of a large part of Europe on the basis of predominantly national States.[1]

National consciousness began to appear in the cosmopolitan world of medieval universities and in the councils of the equally cosmopolitan Catholic Church. Reformation found in the national spirit of some ethnic groups one of its supports. Among Eastern Christian Churches, some (e.g. Armenian, Coptic, Syrian) retained an ethnic character, making of religion a strong supporting element both of the fact of nationality and of a sentiment-laden national consciousness. Others—the Russian, Bulgarian, Rumanian, Serbian—developed at various times an increasingly autocephalous structure precisely because the mother Greek-Orthodox Church was not regarded by worshippers and clergy as sufficiently close from

1. One must be particularly careful in this connection to refrain from misinterpreting history so as to make it fit into the author's favourite scheme. Some authors are fond of ascribing the development of national kingdoms to the pull of nationality only, while ignoring those very real cases where nationalities such as we know them are the result of, rather than the stimulus to, State formations. Others point gleefully to the cases of the latter kind, while neglecting those of the former variety. Both attitudes are one-sided to the extent of not conforming to the minimum requirements that must be observed by anyone who attempts a scholarly treatment of a problem.

an ethnic viewpoint. Judaism, despite its universalistic theology, has hardly ever departed from the path of a mono-ethnic religion, and this strengthened both the fact of and the desire for ethnic coherence among Jews, even though the political implications inherent in this stand were principally turned into mystical and eschatological channels.[1]

Certain long-drawn-out armed conflicts, such as the series of wars between Christians and Moslems in Spain, between Russians and their neighbours on the east, south and west, and the Hundred Years' War across France, did much to arouse national consciousness among those concerned, and it was this consciousness that played a significant part in the formation of what may objectively be regarded as a Spanish, a Russian, a French nation. Similarly, the resentment of many an educated native of the Apennine peninsula at seeing himself and others of his kind governed by German-speaking or Spanish-speaking rulers had much to do with making him aware of the relative similarity of the inhabitants of the peninsula's cities and provinces and with making him cherish those features which they had in common; thus creating a sentiment of an Italian nation, and the nation itself, out of what might have developed into a group of distinct nations, as indeed happened in the case of the various groups of southern and western Slavs. And while in the case of Spaniards and Russians there was the added element of religious diversity to lend more substance to the

1. To avoid a renascence of the odd dispute on whether Jews have constituted historically a nation and regarded themselves as one it will suffice to note that in all Jewish sources down to the nineteenth century the Jewish community is predominantly identified as *am Israel*—the nation (or: people) of Israel. The controversy on this point did not arise until the end of the eighteenth century when the idea of an ethnic basis for a political community became fairly common among the educated European élite. To escape the implication that Jewish hetero-ethnicity involves a distinct political status, thus endangering the civic emancipation of Jews, the slogan was raised that Jews were 'merely a religious group'. Many Jews, indeed, took up this attitude, while others, strongly stimulated by the hostile attitude of non-Jews, adopted a deliberately national-minded stand and sought political status either as a national minority or, by way of Zionism, as a territorially organized group ultimately formed into the State of Israel.

contrast between them and their antagonists, the resulting group-consciousness was not only religiously motivated but also ethnically motivated. The groups that came out of the process were not merely Catholic or Greek-Orthodox but also Spaniards and Russians. In the remaining cases of the French and Italians the element of religious diversity from their antagonists was, of course, absent. We see, then, that even the supposedly modern phenomenon of nationalism, the conscious will to be a nation, *preceding* the objective existence of a nation, has important precedents in the past.

Humanism and the renaissance, followed by the related doctrines of liberalism, rationalism and utilitarianism, and finally by socialism, all presented the Occident with sets of values capable of exercising great attraction. Each of them focused attention either on the individual or on a different and larger group than a mere nation, thus reducing preoccupation with the national phenomenon and detracting from its value. These ideologies must be regarded, therefore, as factors working against nationalism. They continue working in this manner to this very day, and so do other ideologies—the old inter- and supra-national religions, the newly powerful cosmopolitan vision of a politically and culturally united humanity, and, to some extent still, the purely State- or dynasty-oriented attitude. None the less, since the beginning of the nineteenth century nationalism has grown tremendously in the world, rising from a creed held mainly among part of the social élites in not too large a part of the world along with other creeds held by them to the position of a veritable mass movement that engulfed most of the world. Observers may disagree about the desirability or otherwise of nationalism, but there is no gainsaying its force: most of the important changes that have occurred in the political map of the world in the course of the past 150 years and most of the new States that have been formed during this period must be ascribed to a major extent to its influence.

Two principal reasons account for the relative weakness of nationalism during most of the course of history. On the one hand, the relative immobility of the large masses of mankind, coupled with their lack of literacy, kept their outlook geared to the immediate social group with which they experienced close personal contact (the village, the clan, the tribe), thus making them regard as strangers those who, though belonging in a larger sense to the same ethnic group, lived beyond these narrow confines. On the other hand, loyalties during these long periods of history, if at all transcending the limits of the personal-contact group, were engaged on the basis of common religion or of dynastic tradition more often than on an ethnic basis. If rulers belonged to an ethnic group different from that of their subjects this mattered but little to most of the latter. The social gulf that divided them was so wide anyhow that the added distinction did not essentially change the picture. Indeed, at times this gulf contributed to the semi-mystic aura which often enveloped rulers during the periods described and thus helped to legitimize their rule. As we have seen, exceptions to this state of affairs abound since early times; but these exceptions are found among peoples with greater than average mobility, a better than average education; among those who, on account of the small size of their territory located within a relatively densely populated area, came into frequent mass contact with other ethnic groups; or among those who experienced such contact in conflict situations. In these conditions, and among élite groups for which these conditions prevailed, the relative similarities among the members of a single nation stood out in comparison with the dissimilarities offered by other nations, thus lifting the fact to the level of consciousness, engaging empathy and antipathy and making possible an incipient nationalism.

With the renaissance and the reformation, mankind in Europe becomes generally more mobile in a physical sense, and its intellectual horizons broaden, embracing greater knowledge of other and different nations and stimulating perception of the difference.[1] At the same time the role of religion as a

1. To a certain extent the beginning of this process can be traced to the Crusades, and, indeed, manifestations of nationalism are found among crusaders both in Europe and in the Orient. However, the very strong bonds of a common religious endeavour overshadowed the national factor at that time and held it in check.

common reference-point of political loyalties weakens, while dynastic and feudal allegiance as ultimate justification of a political entity is increasingly displaced by the idea of the 'natural' right of people to be governed in accordance with their wishes.

From there to the nineteenth-century 'principle of nationalities', i.e. the principle according to which each nationality has a valid claim to statehood, is a transition that can be, and indeed was, achieved in a few easy stages. It is quite plausible that people, when consulted about the kind of rule under which they wish to live, will not wish to be governed by *strangers* to their *mores* nor to have *strange values* imposed upon them. Democratic thinking serves thus to reinforce nationalism wherever a ruling group is ethnically different from the mass of the governed, and this is a situation which has confronted a very appreciable part of the human race in recent centuries. As a result of these developments, consciousness of one's nationality assumed in the Western world the character of a permanent and mass phenomenon rather than of a sporadic and isolated one, and was increasingly linked with the attribution of a positive value to the preservation of that nationality both in the cultural and in the political spheres. The French Revolution having brought the democratic idea to a culmination point, the Napoleonic conquests, with their attempt to subject anew various European nationalities to 'alien' rule, unleash a violent reaction. Resistance to this attempt is based, as far as the mass of the populations involved and especially their educated strata is concerned, not on the old principle of *legitimacy* but on the new principle now known as *nationalism*.

Modern nationalism appears therefore at first as an extension of liberal and democratic ideas and as their application, beyond the individual, to the entire ethnic group with which the individual regards himself as linked. Where liberal democracy demands a political structure in which the individual, together with his peers, determines the regime under which he is to live and expects such regime to grant him the utmost opportunities for self-expression consistent with other established community goals, nationalism adds the demand that the sum total of individuals constituting an ethnic group be given collectively a similar right, again with the expectation that the resulting regime will offer maximum opportunities for self-expression and growth to those values which the members of the group hold in common, i.e. to national values. Democratic self-government becomes in this context 'national self-determination', and liberty becomes 'national freedom'. In this liberal-democratic context nationalism is still a universalistic idea claiming that national self-determination and national freedom be applied to all nations. Thus understood, nationalism has triumphed in nineteenth-century Europe under the name of the 'principle of nationalities'. And it was still on the basis of the same premises that the idea has spread in recent decades to the Middle East and to the colonial areas in Africa, Asia and Oceania and the non-self-governing regions of America and the West Indies. Strengthened in these parts by colour differences between rulers and ruled, the idea of ethnic self-determination has played a dominant part in the process of de-colonization, often before even the consciousness of national cohesion has overcome narrower tribal or local loyalties among the population and before a wider ethnic unity has in fact emerged from a collection of fairly isolated tribal, village or clan-based communities. As earlier in Europe, the educated strata were the first to take up the trend.

On the other hand, the strong emotional emphasis on the values of *one's own* nationality, inseparable from any national-minded or nationalist movement and essential in order to overcome the obstacles in its way, may end by distorting the universalistic implications of the concept. This emphasis leads adherents of a national movement all too often to adopt the view that, should contradictions develop between the interests of one's own nationality and those of other nationalities, the latter may and should be sacrificed to the former irrespective of their relative merits. Thus nationalism assumes its second face of a movement bent externally on aggression and internally on domination, discrimination, forcible assimilation or total exclusion of other ethnic groups. In the same manner the strong emotional absorption in advancing *national* values may tend to push aside the other values involved in the movement's liberal and democratic background. Freedom of the individual, including his freedom to choose and change his leaders, may come to be regarded as secondary to the exigencies of the struggle for national independence; then—to the exigencies of maintaining a national independence once won or of furthering other national goals; and finally—to the routine and convenience of a governing group by now accustomed to rule unhindered by liberal and democratic scruples and no longer willing to have its position curtailed.

Recent European history has amply proved that such an undemocratic, illiberal, aggression-bent nationalism, while not a necessary outcome, may quite possibly be the outcome of the process. Available evidence seems to indicate that extra-European nationalisms will be no more immune to this kind of development than their European equivalents. If we take into consideration that extra-European communities, Northern America and the Australian-New Zealand complex excepted, are far less deeply rooted in liberal and democratic traditions than Europe, the probabilities are that in the rest of the world nationalism will prove even more prone to assume an undemocratic, illiberal, aggression-bent aspect.

It remains to examine somewhat more closely the circumstances which favour or hinder the development of nationalism as well as to assay its strength and intensity, in comparison to other ideological motivations in human society. We have already seen that it is contact with members of other ethnic groups which is a pre-condition for grasping the differences between them and one's own ethnic group, and therefore for the conception that the latter group, despite sectional and other differences within it, forms a relative unit. Since ethnic and national consciousness is the first ingredient of nationalism we may say that both develop best where such inter-ethnic contacts are most frequent. A possibly anecdotal poll alleged to have been conducted by students in some Russian universities early in the present century serves to dramatize the point. According to the tale,[1] a group of students, wishing to test self-identification within the population, arranged to stop passers-by in different cities of Russia, asking them the deliberately vague question: 'What are you?' In the cities of the interior, where the population was almost entirely Russian by nationality, the usual answer is said to have been: 'I am a carpenter, a peasant, a merchant, a teacher', etc. In the western provinces, where the population was ethnically mixed to a large degree, the replies went mostly: 'I am a Russian, a Pole, a German, a Jew, a Lithuanian', etc. Whether true or not, the story purports to emphasize the difference between belonging in fact to an ethnic unit and having this fact brought to the forefront of one's consciousness to an extent where it will overshadow certain other social links.

The real point at issue, to which the story quoted pretends to furnish a partial answer, concerns the question: how does close proximity of ethnic groups affect the *fact*, the *consciousness* and the *positive evaluation* of belonging to a given nationality? The answer to the question is by no means as unequivocal as might appear from the story. On the level of fact, experience demonstrates that close proximity quite often results, in members of a non-dominant ethnic group, in a toning down of their identifying group characteristics in favour of those of the dominant ethnic group, leading to their gradual submergence in the latter. This process is traditionally known as *assimilation* to, and is more recently referred to as *integration* with, the dominant group. In other cases such proximity has led to the gradual toning down of the distinguishing features of all or most pre-existing ethnic groups and their merger into a new nationality, new because its characteristics are not sufficiently close to those of any pre-existing group to allow us to identify the two. And, again, cases are known where despite long proximity a fairly strong maintenance of ethnic peculiarities and identities of the

1. The story was related to the present writer by the late Professor Max Laserson, of the University of St Petersburg and later of Columbia University. The writer has been unable to find any other reference to, or corroboration of, the story. Its authenticity must therefore be strongly doubted.

various ethnic groups may be observed. Paralleling these variations, proximity accompanied by intermingling may either lower or even atrophy altogether ethnic consciousness or, on the contrary, intensify it to the point illustrated in our story. Modern France can be cited as an outstanding example of the submergence of secondary ethnic groups in the dominant one. The emergence of the Italian nation during the Middle Ages illustrates best the merger of various groups into a new composite nationality. The United States and the republics of Latin America are at present undergoing a process very closely resembling such emergence of new composite nationalities, but in their cases the culture of one ethnic component—the English, Spanish and Portuguese respectively—exercises an influence so much stronger than those of the other components that they may well be considered an intermediate category. The maintenance of separate ethnic identities and sentiments despite proximity is amply demonstrated all over Central and Eastern Europe, the Near East and Ceylon. Again, the cases mentioned here are illustrative of general trends only. Within each of the countries named we shall find differentials in the intensity or speed with which various ethnic groups integrate or maintain their identities, and individuals or smaller groups will be found that maintain an attitude contrary to the general trend.

In searching to identify the factors which facilitate either national integration or the maintenance and intensification of national distinctions in conditions of proximity, we would not go wrong in attributing a particularly important influence to the element of inter-ethnic *tension*. Proximity *per se* leads to integration, despite all contrary influences, and in the very long run, if we measure time by centuries and certainly by millennia, this seems to be the final outcome.[1] But wherever

1. We are not concerned at this point with the question whether, in the course of such long periods of time, new factors of *disintegration* may not appear, giving birth to new nationalities. The map of nationalities is shifting in time as well as in space. Some disappear and others are born, and the borders of their habitats are changing too. In this respect nationality is no different from the State.

tensions among ethnic groups are strong at any given time, such tensions slow down the integration process and set in motion a contrary process: awareness of and antagonism to the ethnically different group grow, awareness of and sentimental attachment to one's own group intensify, and at the point where this leads to wide-spread political claims on an ethnic basis we are confronted by nationalism.

It is an accepted tenet of modern thinking that tension is born out of frustrated expectations. In the sphere of inter-ethnic relations a frustrated ethnic group is one whose expectations *qua* group remain unfulfilled. It is important, therefore, to enquire what circumstances lead an ethnic group to expect that the political structure should be responsive to its characteristics and to develop frustrations should this fail to be the case; or, since expectations are a psychological phenomenon attaching to individual human beings, under what circumstances individual members of an ethnic group will develop expectations of this kind. We have seen already that a basic minimum of democratic thinking—the idea that the composition and major objectives of the ruling group should reflect the people's wishes—enters into the picture. Surveying the course of history as well as the scenes of contemporary developments, we would suggest that a further prime factor in this context is the factor of *individual migration* v. living in the *traditional group habitat*. Other things being equal, members of an ethnic group who migrate, more or less on an individual basis, to an area with an already established ethnic pattern and a political organization not inferior in power to their own, do so mostly in the hope of bettering their condition as individuals, but do not harbour any expectations to re-constitute in a new place a collective habitat for the group as such. On the contrary, the very readiness to leave their traditional group-habitat implies a measure of renunciation to the group-preserving facilities afforded by the former environment. Whatever difficulties of integration to the ethnico-cultural patterns of the new domicile may be experienced by such immigrants, they are due to the characteristic difficulties of individual adjustment to a strange environment; the difficulties will be stronger in the case of older or less educated individuals, weaker in the case of the younger and better-educated ones. But the mass-shared desire on the part of the members of the group to cling to their group-identity and its folkways, to claim for the group a decisive voice in shaping the political structure of society, and to expect that political structure to reflect and further the group's specific values, is no longer there. It may still linger on in the case of some odd members of the group, but these will constitute the exception rather than the rule. With most group members, emigration from their native habitat under such circumstances means renunciation to nationalism as a mass ideology and a mass movement.

With this gone, the attraction of proximity, the pressure of the mass of the population on a minority, will inevitably exercise their leavening influence on the non-dominating group in the direction of integration. This is what happened and continues to happen in countries of mass immigration, such as the American republics, Australia and Canada. On a smaller scale, but no less effectively, we encounter the same phenomenon in other countries where immigrants stream into a developed society with a well-established ethnic profile. The Huguenots in Germany and South Africa, the Scottish and French and Russian *émigrés* who left their countries after major upheavals, the emigrants from Eastern and Southern Europe who found a home in Britain and France, in Belgium and Scandinavia, are only some examples of the kind. We can still observe among them some phenomena of group-consciousness, but these are in the main transitional phenomena pending full integration, and are concerned with less ambitious aims: with assuring non-discrimination to the members of the immigrant group, with their rise in the economic and social scale and with their adequate representation within the political and occupational élites. At last, nothing remains but a faint sentimental attachment to the ancestral habitat and to certain cultural or folkloristic peculiarities of the nationality whence some or all of the individual's ancestors may have sprung. Even this remnant differs in intensity from case to case, being generally stronger in the New World, with its faintly pluralistic atmosphere, than in the more uniform atmosphere of the countries of Western and Northern Europe.[1]

This generalization holds good only where a certain fairly complex set of conditions actually obtains. These conditions comprise a country of immigration which enjoys a relatively advanced degree of technological development, possesses a political organization acknowledged as such by the prevailing powers in the international community and sufficiently strong to impose itself on the immigrants, is fairly densely inhabited, and the mass of whose inhabitants have reached a degree of ethnic integration tantamount to their crystallization into a nation. A further condition is that this dominant nation and its ruling group on the one hand, and the immigrants on the other, exhibit a reasonable readiness to allow for the immigrants' integration on terms that would not be too onerous or humiliating to either side. Where one or more of these features are lacking, the ensuing picture may differ very considerably. If the ethnic character of the country is not yet stabilized on the basis of a well-crystallized dominant nationality, large-scale immigration, rather than resulting in the submergence of the immigrants in that nationality, may result in a merger of the different ethnic groups, newcomers and old-timers alike, into a new composite nation. This is what happened indeed over a large part of medieval Europe at the time its now existing nationalities were formed; to some extent a similar phenomenon has been characteristic of the as yet uncompleted process of nationality formation in the republics of North and South America; and something similar may yet be the outcome

1. This difference might have been attributed to the difference in the weight of numbers, since immigrants to the New World tend to concentrate in large numbers in a given area and are therefore presumably more resistant to complete integration. However, groups such as Russians in Paris, Italians, Poles and Spaniards in certain parts of France, Czechs in Vienna and Italians in London have shown a similar pattern of settlement, and yet after very few generations even the limited sentimental folkloristic attachment to the ancestral nation tends there to disappear completely. A merely numerical explanation would not seem, therefore, to do justice to the complexities involved.

of the melting-pots of formerly British East Africa, of Malaya and of Singapore.

Similarly, if the immigration movement is systematically organized and politically sponsored rather than sporadic and individual, or if the immigrants bear a consciousness of their cultural, social or economic superiority to the native population, they will deliberately aim at maintaining their ethnic identity and, if possible, at securing for that group the position of a dominant nationality in the area. The phenomenon encountered here is that which has become familiar under the name of *colonization*, in the widest use of the term. The choice of policies available to the would-be dominating immigrant nationality is a very wide one. Its main variations are that of maintaining the ethnic distinction and even the numerical balance between the groups while relegating the autochthonous population to a secondary role economically and socially as well as politically, and that of making the immigrant nationality pre-eminent in numbers as well as in position. In the first case we deal with colonialism in the narrower sense, with the type that used to be known as 'planters' colonies', in which a relatively thin upper stratum of colonists and their descendants set themselves up as rulers and economic masters of the native population. In the second case we deal with an organized attempt on the part of the immgrants and the powers behind them to *enlarge* the national habitat rather than to leave it behind; and sometimes the new territory will loom in the eyes of the immigrants as affording opportunities to establish a better, more perfect, group-habitat than the original home ever was, with conditions more auspicious for the advancement of the group, and not only of the individual migrants and their families. Both varieties leave room for a great many shadings and nuances in their attitudes towards hetero-ethnic elements, ranging from a fair degree of readiness to absorb some or all of such elements, through several degrees of leniency or severity in the treatment of hetero-ethnic groups, and down to mass expulsion or even mass extermination of the native stock. Without going back to antiquity, it will suffice to mention the German colonization of Slavonic and Baltic regions beginning with the early Middle

Ages, the Crusader States in the Orient, the expansion of the Polish gentry into Ukrainian, Russian and Lithuanian territory, that of the Russians into territories to the east and south of their original area of settlement, and, finally, the colonial ventures of Western European nations across the seas and the oceans. Over and above the countless variations of colonial policy carried on in these instances, they are characterized by the common denominator of a desire to secure a broader basis for the nation that sent out its colonists rather than by the immigrants' readiness to forego their traditional ethnic identity and loyalties; this is so even if in some significant cases (the Boers of South Africa, Canada, the United States, the Spanish and Portuguese colonists in Latin America, Australia) the changed environment and other factors have led to the evolution of new nationalities.

In some cases a group of immigrants, rightly or wrongly conscious of their superiority, has been able to maintain its ethnic identity over long periods of time in a relatively underdeveloped environment even if not supported by political and military factors and even if not moved by far-reaching political motives. The German settlements in the Volga region, in southern Russia and in the Banat are the best-known examples of this kind. Another factor that slows down the ethnic integration of immigrants is a religious denomination which appears as strongly nonconformist in relation to the denomination or denominations current among the native population. But of particular importance as a slowing-down factor is a deliberate policy of a country's rulers, or an attitude among the masses of its population, or a combination of both, which is averse to the immigrants' full integration. Such an attitude of rejection or non-receptiveness on the part of the native stock and its rulers, whatever its motives or reasons, may result in the retention by the immigrants of the consciousness of their ethnic identity and in its intensification to the point where it assumes the familiar forms of a politically oriented nationalism. Colour distinctions have been particularly prone to stimulate this attitude of non-receptiveness or outright rejection, while within the white 'race' Jews have been singled out particularly for such treatment, and this phenomenon helps to explain the maintenance of the ethnic identity and the revival of nationalism among so many Jews despite the manifold migratory movements they underwent in the course of a long history. We see, therefore, that in the final analysis readiness to integrate or to be integrated, and its opposite, when exhibited by dominant and by non-dominant groups, by immigrants and by the host groups, serve as major qualifying factors in connection with the generalization offered before, and according to which migration, other things being equal, constitutes a counter-indication to nationalism.

Still, the main forum of a nationalism-breeding inter-ethnic tension is a territory claimed with some reason as the historical habitat, or the homeland, by more than one nationality. This is why Europe, with its many disputed border areas and its ethnically mixed population, has become the classical arena of ethnic tensions and, consequently, of nationalism. The environment, with its multitude of symbols and associations linking the territory to a given nationality, stimulates attachment to that nationality's values and intensifies the individual's resolve to strengthen both his bonds with the group and the future outlook for the group itself. The facts and legends of the nation's past reinforce the desire to equal or surpass that grandeur in the future. Any shortcomings or indignities suffered by the group in the present only sharpen this desire. And the fact that the obstacles to the attainment of this aim can only too often be identified with human agents connected with a different nationality imbues the resulting nationalism with a competitive spirit which serves, first, to set in motion a movement of national liberation and which may, once this goal is achieved, nurture still more ambitious projects of aggrandizement. In these conditions, despite the integrating influence of proximity and intermingling, and while nationalism and nationality-denying integration[1] are both taking place, it was

1. One should be careful not to confuse all integration with a denial of nationalism. When a non-dominant ethnic group, in Europe usually also a numerical minority, integrates with the dominant nationality, its members do not forswear nationality-consciousness and nationalism as such. They renounce nationalism on the basis of their former ethnic connections, only

nationalism that has, since the beginning of the nineteenth century, produced the more spectacular effects. Switzerland is about the one major instance in which nationalities, while 'rubbing shoulders' in conditions of extreme proximity and common political rule, have succeeded in reducing ethnic tension to a minimum; the state of equilibrium reached by them and carefully balanced between a de-nationalizing integration and a self-assertive nationalism seems to have left all of Switzerland's nationalities reasonably satisfied. It will be seen later that certain indications in present-day Europe permit us to hope that a similar relaxation of tensions, a similar equilibrium, may yet develop among other nationalities, thus allowing for their peaceful co-existence and for the taming of nationalism. But if we observe nineteenth-century Europe, the immediate predecessor of the present-day continent, we may say that, with the exception of Switzerland, it could be divided, like ancient Gaul, into three major categories. On the one hand we had nationalities many of whose members regarded their political status as unsatisfactory because they lived in a State dominated by a different nationality and the latter exploited this domination either in order to enforce integration or in order to arrogate to itself special privileges, or both. To this category belonged the Irish, the Icelanders, the Norwegians, the Flemish in Belgium, the Danes and Poles and Alsatians and Lotharingians in post-1871 Germany, all non-German nationalities in Austria, all non-Magyar nationalities in Hungary, non-Russian nationalities in Russia, non-Turkish nationalities in the Ottoman Empire, first the Finns and later the Swedes in Finland, and sundry non-dominating nationalities in the Balkan States after their separation from Turkey. On the margin of this category there were several ethnic groups with incipient ethnic-political frustrations that, however, fell short of developing into significant political problems and most of

to be caught and swallowed up within a generation or two in the nationalism of the dominant nationality which they have joined. This 'majority nationalism' is, of course, closely linked to the traditional State structure and is therefore palatable to many an observer who rejects 'minority nationalism'.

which are undergoing a peaceful process of dissolution: Welsh, Scots, Lapps, Frisians, Bretons, Savoyards, Corsicans.

A second category was composed of groups that considered themselves splinters of a wider nationality and that, while dominant each in a given State, lived in States which did not encompass the entire nationality, a situation that led to a feeling of dissatisfaction. Under this heading we should mention Germans before 1871 and, if we consider the 'Greater Germany' trend in Austria and the Sudeten area, at a later period as well; Italians before 1871 and, if we remember Trieste, until 1918; Serbs between 1878 and 1918; Bulgarians between 1878 and 1908; Greeks until 1914 and in a certain sense up to now; Arabs in an incipient manner before the disappearance of the Ottoman Empire and to a more pronounced degree after the First and especially after the Second World Wars. To the third category belong those nations which had succeeded at an earlier period, either by design or by accident of history, in becoming the dominant ethnic factor in a sovereign State that englobed in its population the quasi-totality of the nation's membership, and whose only remaining nationalist ambition is to solve satisfactorily relations with hetero-ethnic groups in their midst, on their borders, or beyond the borders.

Within all three of these groups of nationalities differing formulations of nationalist goals have been evolved, modest or radical in their expectations depending on circumstances. Nationalist movements among the first two groups invariably sought solutions visualizing a change of the existing political *status quo*. Nationalism of the third variety sometimes sought satisfaction on the basis of the existing *status quo* (British and French colonial policies after 1920; the Dutch; the Swedes; the Hungarians until the final stages of the First World War; by and large the Russians and Turks both before and after their crucial national revolutions), sometimes by expansion across the borders either in contingent territories or overseas (the British and French before 1920; Russians before 1878; Italians after the unification of Italy, first sporadically, and—during the fascist period—systematically; Germans 1871–1918 and 1933–45). It should be remembered, of course, that in this third group of nations there existed a high degree of identification between their political and their ethnic structures, causing them to identify the two in their consciousness as well; consequently their ventures, whether of a conservationist or of an expansionist nature, are often undertaken on behalf of the State and in the name of a 'reason of State' rather than under the name of nationalism. This has led even acute observers in the countries in question to lull themselves into the belief that ethnic nationalism was altogether absent in their cases. It is only when dealing with hetero-ethnic elements subject to the rule of a State of the latter variety that the essential difference between the State and its dominant nationality becomes *occasionally* perceptible and that an ethnically oriented nationalism appears from under the cloak of a State-minded patriotism.

Both the intensity and the effectiveness of nationalism are far from being solely determined by the fact of proximity and by the varieties of subjection, discrimination and non-discrimination encountered by the nation's members. Ideologies, i.e. comprehensive sets of values formulated for the guidance of human beings, when current among members of a given national group, play a crucial role in furthering or toning down nationalist reactions to these facts. If a set of values is widely accepted within a group of people which attaches central importance to other-than-ethnic links—whether religious, dynastic, class-oriented, cosmopolitan-humanistic, individualistic, ethical, grossly materialistic, hedonistic and so forth—inter-ethnic relationships which, under different circumstances, might have led to acute frustrations, strong tensions and pronounced nationalist reactions, may fail to produce these results. On the other hand, where the ethnic group and its characteristics have become the objects of a strongly positive evaluation, even minor frustrations easily arouse intense nationalist reactions. Now, in the diffusion of ideologies, the influence of élites is uppermost, and therefore the growth of nationalism, too, can be traced in a large measure to the influence of those élites which, having themselves become attracted to nationalist values, were able to spread them among larger groups. Herein lies the grain of truth contained in the often-repeated assertion of scholars of the Actonian school who harp on the 'artificial' nature of nationalism. What they fail to see, however, is that this kind of 'artificiality' is nothing exceptional. The same assertion could be made of State patriotism, of religious loyalty, of class solidarity, of democratic doctrine, of morality, of the concept of man's inalienable or natural rights; in brief, of any ideology or social philosophy which ever got hold of any segment of mankind. Only, the ideology of nationalism having begun its victorious march later than most of them, it has appeared to a number of adherents of the older and more familiar ideologies as a presumptuous and somewhat illegitimate *parvenu.*

Placing in its proper perspective the ideological factor in the march of nationalism will help us to understand the somewhat paradoxical part which literacy, higher education and technological advance have played in that development. It might have been expected that education, once it has overcome the initial stage of focusing the individual's attention beyond his immediate social environment and on the wider national group, would broaden man's horizon and turn both his attention and his loyalties into channels more universal than those of a single nationality. Pursuing this reasoning, one might have expected that the educated élite of a nation would take the lead in this direction and would be farthest away from nationalism. Then again, the more technological advance and the related phenomena of a higher economic level and of mass-communication media intensify contacts between national groups and standardize their formerly distinct characteristics, one would expect nationalism to decline. In fact the effect of these factors is by no means that simple. In many cases such manifestations can indeed be observed. Some of mankind's leading spirits have had no patience with that relatively narrow reference-point of human loyalties represented by the nation and sought larger, less divisive, foci of loyalty. Possibly more of that will occur in the future. Similarly, further advancement in economic well-being, in technological skills and in mass media may indeed result in a growing diminution both of national diversities and of the value attached to these diversities. The 'Americanization' observable all over the world—communist countries included—in the middle of the present century and the already mentioned growth of a 'common European spirit' among the nations of Europe may be taken as likely precursors of future developments. Nevertheless, the spread of education and of technical progress hitherto has on the balance strengthened rather than weakened nationalist trends, and the educated élite has been the spearhead in this development. This has been the case in Europe and this is the case presently in Africa and Asia. Indeed, the conquest of these continents by nationalist doctrines has been following the spread of Western educational standards and is part of their conquest by the totality of modern ideologies that have originated in the West. Once more it is the intellectuals who are found in the forefront of the movement.

The spread of literacy and of mass-communication media has done more than further nationalism. It has also *speeded up* the time-span required to produce the result. It now takes less time to reach masses with new ideologies and symbols, and the frequency and intensity with which the masses can be reached are also greatly increased. To indoctrinate existing nations with nationalism now takes less time than ever before, and so does it take less time to produce new nations by the process of integration. A similar speed-up, and for similar reasons, can be observed in the process of de-nationalizing members of non-dominant nationalities, but since the ultimate result of that process is usually their integration into a dominant or newly created composite nationality, it is nationality that appears as the main beneficiary of the acceleration. Where several generations were needed in earlier periods to produce national integration of smaller social units, to crystallize national characteristics and to stimulate national consciousness, the powerful impact of concentrated modern methods of indoctrination and propaganda makes it possible to achieve these results in one or two generations. The fires of history burn fiercer in our days, temperatures are raised quicker, and the slow stewing-pot of history, in which nations used to acquire leisurely their distinct flavours, has been replaced by a pressure-cooker which accomplishes the job in a fraction of the time.

Last but not least, the influence of foreign political factors on the development of nationalism may not be ignored. Propaganda in favour of national consciousness is quite often directed at ethnic groups from across a political border, and it would be the acme of naiveté to ascribe such propaganda to sentiments of ethnic solidarity or to adherence to the principle of nationalities either alone or necessarily. Quite often it is the political advantage of the forces behind the propaganda machine that is aimed at, the principal forms of such advantage being the direct aggrandizement of the State concerned, the increase of its indirect influence and the weakening of a possibly antagonistic State. No less pronounced is the effect of the attitude of foreign States, similarly motivated, on the chances of a nationalist movement succeeding to carry its objectives to fruition. In the granting of collective rights to the Christian minority nations in the Ottoman Empire and the subsequent extension of the minorities protection system after the First World War, the pressure of the leading Powers of the day played a far greater part than the pressures engendered by the minority groups themselves. Similarly, the non-adoption of this form of minorities protection in Western countries and its general decline after the Second World War in favour of the principle of individual equality are again due to the attitudes of the leading Powers.[1] Still more pronounced is the influence of foreign States as an active agent for the advancement or retardation of the demand of nationalities for changes in the

1. The principal cases in which collective rights of national minorities on a personal basis were newly adopted after the Second World War or survived that war—Cyprus, Finland, Israel, Lebanon, the Union of South Africa (as far as the English- and Afrikaans-speaking groups are concerned)—are the result of internal factors in the countries concerned rather than of external factors. This is true also of bilinguism and similar devices on a predominantly territorial basis, and of federalism, for the purpose of affording a modicum of satisfaction to ethnic groups, such as we find in different forms in Belgium, Canada, Switzerland, the Soviet Union and Yugoslavia.

political map of the world. Hardly any movement of secession or of unification of States has ever succeeded without being supported by a favourable foreign political constellation. At that, few and far between were the cases where such foreign political pressures were more than a supporting element added to a genuine national movement.[1] And, of course, major changes in the political map of the world are usually due in part to the intervention of foreign States even when the national motive is lacking, as witness the success of the American revolution with the aid of France and that of Latin American independence movements with the support of the United States and of Great Britain.

Where nationalism has manifested itself, its strength as a social force need not be measured by those successes only which it has registered in competition against non-congenial State structures. It can also be perceived by comparing it with other social forces. We all know how potent an influence economic self-interest exercises in human affairs, and, as a matter of fact, economic self-interest often seizes upon national differences as a welcome justification and magnifies such differences as a means to further its ends. It is also a familiar fact that depression intensifies national antagonisms. However, where economic self-interest enters in conflict with nationalism, nationalism has usually proved the stronger. An example will suffice.

The city of Danzig was a second-rate port in Germany gradually losing in importance up to 1918. It was then detached from Germany and made a free city, fully autonomous in its internal affairs, but under such arrangements that it became the principal port for Poland, a country with about 30,000,000 inhabitants. Its population grew from 170,000 in 1910 to 266,000 in 1938. Its shipping grew from 3,500 ships with 1,000,000 net tons in 1912 to 6,600 ships with 4,770,000 net tons in 1938. Across the border in Germany the Danzigers saw unemployment for a considerable number of years. Within

1. The creation of Albania in 1913 and that of Iraq and Jordan in successive stages after the First and the Second World Wars can be cited among the few relevant examples.

there was sustained prosperity and assurance of continued growth. And yet the overwhelming majority of Danzigers kept straining at the leash for years trying to achieve reunion with Germany, irrespective of the political regime in that country, until they got their wish in 1939. Undoubtedly they were profoundly influenced by propaganda, but the significant thing is that this propaganda could succeed when economic self-interest pointed so flagrantly the other way.

Similar attachment to national ties at the expense of economic interests was shown bv the inhabitants of Memel, the Saar and Trieste before and after the First World War, and by the Greek majority in Cyprus after the Second World War. But these examples are drawn from a zone where nationalism was at its strongest at the time. It is even more interesting to take a look at the historical encounter between the two great dynamic forces of our time, nationalism and socialism, when the two met as rivals.

Many of the founders of modern socialism, and Marx in particular, had no true conception of the place of nationality in society. In their simplified, utterly materialistic picture of society, nationality was the same sort of semi-artificial product of ballyhoo which some American (who, for all their militant anti-socialism, share the primitive Marxian belief that the key to all of the world's problems lies in economics) and—for other reasons—some British observers still believe it to be. Needless to say, wherever socialism penetrated into lands where nationalism had arrived, this superficial attitude had to give way. In countries such as Poland and Czechoslovakia, in the Russian and Austrian empires, separate socialist parties were formed by each of the different nationalities. Decreasing the emphasis on nationalism and concentrating on economic reform, these socialist parties were able to get along far better than non-socialist parties of the same nationalities; but still—national differences were not eliminated altogether by the common profession of a socialist creed. On the contrary, socialism gradually recognized the opportunity for gaining strength by enlisting the support of underprivileged national groups. Thence proceeds the well-known sympathy between the various shades of socialism and the coloured races of the world. Indeed, it is still an open question whether the alliance between the two will result in socialism climbing to power on the shoulders of national frustrations, whether a harmonious balance between socialism and nationalism is to be achieved by the formerly subject and colonial peoples, or whether, in the end, it won't be nationalism that will come out on top, having made socialism perform its supporting role. In Europe, too, the very formulae of national self-determination and of the protection of national minorities, so well known since their adoption by President Woodrow Wilson, originate in their modern form with the socialist leaders of the old Austrian Empire, who, caught in the maelstrom of nationalism, realized that unless they advocated the free development of nationalities their movement would stand no chance.[1]

But the most significant process took place in the Soviet Union. The leaders of the Russian revolution, who, to gain their ends, were not afraid to upset so many ancient and widespread ideas, who took away some of the most cherished rights of the individual, who did not hesitate to offend public opinion both at home and abroad, saw fit to bow to the principle of nationalities. They did so possibly with their tongues in their cheeks, hoping that some day the nationalities will give up their distinct existence and cautiously working towards this end; but to this day they keep the form and much of the substance of this principle, and the Soviet Union has remained structurally a federation of nationalities.

We thus see that neither mass literacy nor technological development, neither capitalist prosperity nor socialist planning, have succeeded in undermining the importance of nationalism. On the contrary, never was nationalism so outspoken, so expansive a force, as it is in the twentieth century. There is no point in trying to ignore this force or in belittling

1. We purposely abstain from citing as an added proof of socialism's weakness vis-à-vis nationalism the often-mentioned failure of socialism hitherto to stem national unity in war by appealing to international proletarian solidarity. We do so because in this instance socialism is usually confronted by the joint forces of patriotism and nationalism.

it. It is legitimate, however, to examine its workings and to explore the possibilities of taming its power.

Nationalism, when confronted with a State structure not regarded as congenial to national values, and especially when aided by a favourable international constellation, has been able, then, to bring about a radical change in the State structure or even secession and dismemberment of the uncongenial State. It is not necessarily overwhelming physical force that is required in such cases to break the State bonds; cases are known where the result has been achieved by diplomatic pressure from the outside, by fairly passive forms of disaffection on the part of the population concerned, by the weight of wide-spread public opinion, by the weakening of the will to rule under the impact of fashionable ideologies and by a loosening of the State's organizational framework following upon military defeat or an internal revolution. Either of these circumstances may suffice to weaken the bonds that bind a self-conscious national group to a State which it does not regard as 'its own'. A brief list of the States which fell victims to that process since the beginning of the nineteenth century includes the pre-1806 Holy Roman Empire, the Netherlands, the pre-1918 Austro-Hungarian monarchy, the numerous formerly sovereign States of Germany and Italy, the Ottoman Empire, Sweden, the Russian Empire,[1] the Papal State and—with special reference to overseas territories—all colonial

1. The monarchy in Russia was swept away by a revolution that had little or nothing to do with the poly-ethnicity of the country's population. Still, a considerable part of the disaffected elements who laid the groundwork of the revolution came from the ranks of national minorities, and the subsequent falling away of the territorially concentrated minority nationalities in the border areas was a direct result of the doctrine of nationalities, rampant among them and reluctantly assented to by the leaders of the Russian ethnic group as well. The later process of re-gathering these nationalities into a single structure, accomplished in two stages—in 1920–3 and in 1939–44—was mainly a matter of military might and had to be paid for at the cost of an ethnically based federalism. The price was not negligible and represented the only major departure from the 'centralist' practices of Soviet communism. At that, separatist trends are still in existence and explain many of the Soviet Government's policies throughout the decades.

Powers which have lost or are in the process of losing control of their colonies in the present century.[1] The States and political structures which, during the same period, have been formed, to a greater or lesser extent, in response to nationalist stimuli, are still more numerous. They include Belgium,[2] autonomous Hungary under the compromise of 1867, the gradually increased autonomies of the other non-German-speaking parts of the Austrian dominions, the succession States of Austria-Hungary after 1918, the North German Union of 1867 and the German Empire of 1871, the gradual unification of Italy begun in 1848 and completed in 1918, the accession of Balkan nations to independence which began in 1827 and was finally achieved in 1913, the emergence of a number of independent Arab-speaking States—also a lengthy process that began with the break-away of parts of northern Africa from the Ottoman Empire in the first half of the nineteenth century and took about 100 years to complete,[3] and the emergence of

1. We do not include in this list the loss of the American colonies by Britain in the eighteenth, nor the loss of Spanish, Portuguese and French colonies in America in the nineteenth-century, for in these cases the independence movements were caused by other than ethnic motivations. On the other hand, in the continuation of that process in the present century (independence movements in the British and Dutch West Indies) the ethnically motivated nationalist motive is already strongly noticeable.

2. Belgium is itself a poly-ethnic State beset with inter-ethnic tensions. However, the 1830 revolution that resulted in the secession of Belgium from the Netherlands was mainly of an ethnic-religious character, with the French-speaking groups playing a major part in the secessionary movement. In this, just as in the other cases here mentioned, there is no gainsaying the importance of foreign political factors without whose support the independence movement might have come to naught.

3. One should be careful not to ascribe a predominantly nationalist character to all stages of this process. In North Africa the break-away was caused mainly by the search for aggrandizement on the part of local rulers (especially in the case of Mehmed Ali in Egypt) and by the search of European Powers for colonies; both furthered by the weakening of the Empire's hold on its outlying possessions. In the 1915–20 developments the search of Powers for colonial possessions and the beginning of an Arab national movement were the twin causes. But the further changes in the political map of the Arabic-speaking world, while still aided by the international situation, are predominantly a reflex of Arab nationalism. This is so despite the fact that certain specific States set up within the area,

Norway, Ireland and Iceland as independent States in 1907, 1921 and 1944 respectively. Then there was the accession to independence of the border regions of Russia after the First World War. The strengthening of the Soviet Union in the early twenties and the complications following upon the Hitler regime in Germany, the Molotov-Ribbentrop agreement in 1939 and the outcome of the Second World War, have all produced far-reaching changes in the situation, and most of the nationalities concerned found their status changed from one of independence to one of limited autonomy within the federated structure of the Soviet Union; however, the basic acknowledgement of their political rights as national groups, once gained in 1917 and after, has remained unchallenged. Israel and Cyprus may be taken as the latest manifestations of politically successful national movements of the European type, though both exhibit special features: the majority group in Cyprus had really aimed at union with Greece and had to accept independence as a substitute; Israel, while located on the Asian continent, is due to a national movement whose centre was in Europe.

Since the Second World War the process of awakening nationalism has no longer Europe as its centre. The dynamism of nationalist movements is now felt more strongly in Asia and Africa, where it seems still to be in its initial stage, while in Europe, conversely, this dynamism appears to be ebbing. These two developments will have to be considered separately in later chapters.

Before leaving this subject of the historical impact of nationalism on political developments it would be well to guard the reader once more against exaggerations. Were one to view modern political history as mainly a function of self-assertive nationalism one would be guilty of just as one-sided and incorrect an attitude as that adopted by that school of authors who regard nationalism as little more than a malevolent invention of some misguided spirits. Indeed, in addition

such as Jordan and Iraq, were originally due to foreign political factors rather than to ethnic movements and that certain other States existing in the region conform to historical rather than to ethnic divisions.

to the long list of States born of or radically transformed by nationalism, there have come into being other States within the last two centuries which are not at all due to that factor. The most important of the group are the United States of America and the countries of Latin America. In these instances the independence movement—of the mass of the population in the United States, of an upper stratum in the case of Latin America—was a territorially rather than ethnically circumscribed call for self-government based on the democratic ideas of the period and provoked by the severity of a non-representative central government. Other States in the same group are the formerly 'white' dominions of the British Empire and now members of the Commonwealth—Australia, Canada, New Zealand[1]—which have achieved this status without having to go through a violent struggle with the pre-existing State authorities. The 'Congo-State', created by international fiat in 1885, need hardly be taken seriously in this context, since the 'State' was in this case nothing else but a synonym for a personally held colony. But Albania, when created in 1913, also owed next to nothing to any indigenous national movement, being purely a product of balance-of-power politics. It has already been pointed out that the particular delineation of certain Arab States after the Second World War was also due to other than nationalist or even to minor ethnic considerations. Finally, the post-Second World War era gave us the States of Communist and Nationalist China, of North and South Korea, of Western and Eastern

1. A case apart is the Union of South Africa, where the juxtaposition of two well-defined major ethnic groups within the ruling racial group has resulted in a nationality conflict on the European model against the background of a subject hetero-racial majority. Only the Dutch-speaking 'Afrikaners', though, have adopted the nomenclature and slogans of European nationalism; the English-speaking ethnic group, clinging to British usage, has shied away from them.

In Canada, of course, a national problem has arisen and has received a specific solution. But the emergence of Canada as a self-governing dominion and later as an independent State within the Commonwealth has come about on a territorial rather than on an ethnic basis, even though the existence of the 'provinces' has opened opportunities for ethnico-political influence since the beginning.

Germany, of North and South Vietnam—units created by international politics and by the clash of ideologies, and the existence of which, far from being due to nationalist impulses, runs directly counter to them. For all we know, more State-formations of this kind may emerge in the future.

6

The integrationist pattern

LET us take the case, familiar to readers in England and many another country from their own experience, of a State the institutions and policies of which reflect in the main the *mores* and outlook prevalent in a single ethnic group. Such a State may, however this may have come about, be at present mono-ethnic in the composition of its population, or else it may number among its inhabitants, in addition to the dominant ethnic group, subjects belonging to other ethnic groups, but these would occupy a definitely secondary position and may even be made to suffer from mild or severe forms of discrimination.[1] In the latter case, too, it is not the values, the *mores*, the language, of the secondary groups that will give the State its specific physiognomy, but the values, the *mores*, the language, of the dominant ethnic group or, at the very least, those adopted by that group's social and cultural élite. These standards need not, and under modern conditions are most unlikely to, have been evolved in isolation. They can be often traced to foreign influences of either remote or recent origin. Witness such crucial influences as the penetration of the Phoenician alphabet and its Greek and Latin derivatives into the West, the Chinese alphabet in Japan, the Arabic alphabet in the Near and Middle East, Greek and Roman political institutions, Jewish and Roman concepts of law and justice,

1. To simplify matters, we omit the role played by temporary inhabitants—traders, missionaries, scientists, technicians or simply tourists—on the development of any given national culture. It should be remembered, however, that this role can be quite decisive.

Persian and Hellenistic and Roman administrative patterns and the conquest of the world by Christianity, Islam and Buddhism —each a product of a specific ethnic environment. Witness also such more recent and quite modern influences as the adoption of English as the principal language of cultural and official intercourse in Ireland, India, Burma and a number of African countries, the similar adoption of French in other African States, in Madagascar and in Haiti, or the present-day 'Americanization' that is sweeping the world. But the salient point is that, whatever the origin of the particular feature, it is the adoption of the feature by the leading stratum of an ethnic group as an integral part of the ethnic pattern that is decisive.

When we are in the presence of a State in which the population is more or less mono-ethnic we have before us what is known by the modern expression of a nation-State or, more precisely, a national State. As has been pointed out before, in a State of this kind there is no essential conflict between the basic values of the State and the national values of its only or overwhelmingly dominant nationality, and the two tend to converge in the consciousness of the people. Even if State authorities try to bring about a radical departure from custom-hallowed national patterns, impose new standards, and as a result the paths of State and nation temporarily diverge,[1] this divergence does not stem from a State structure that is ethnically 'foreign' to the population, but springs from elements—however distinct socially and culturally—which are still felt to belong to the same ethnic community. Therefore, even if such attempts should breed serious tensions, these would not be inter-ethnic tensions.

Whether such a nation-State would experience nationalism depends on circumstances. As we have seen earlier, as long as its activities and the daily experience of its population involve

1. Good examples are Peter the Great's reforms in Russia, Ataturk's reforms in Turkey, the Eighteenth (Prohibition) Amendment and perhaps also the de-segregation policy of the United States government and the modernization and social policy of most new States in Asia and Africa.

no appreciable contacts with other nations, the mass of the population and perhaps even its élite may remain relatively unconscious of the character of the ethnic bonds that unite them among themselves and that distinguish them from different ethnic groups. Where such contacts increase, this similarity-dissimilarity pattern will force itself on their consciousness. The chances are that a predominant early reaction to this state of affairs would be a somewhat suspicious and therefore inimical curiosity towards the strangers, the attitude known to us under the name of *xenophobia*—dislike, or fear, of the foreigner. But inasmuch as the ethnically foreign in this situation tend also to be identified with an alien political community, with a foreign State, the ensuing xenophobia would appear as an attitude directed against the stranger's political foreignness as much as against his ethnic foreignness, with the line between the two remaining rather blurred. It goes without saying that major religious divergence contributed a great deal to the feeling of ethnic strangeness, since religion in pre-modern society regulated so much of men's way of life that it inevitably became a major determinant of ethnic identification; accordingly the pre-modern mono-ethnic State is also in most cases a religiously homogeneous State. Similarly, under the conditions described, the inward-directed awareness, the identification of one's own community, would not clearly distinguish in the nation-State between one's ethnic community—the nation, and one's political community—the State. And still the same convergence might characterize the sentimental attachment to, and the purposeful drive to further the interests of, the two entities of nation and State. As a result, nationalism (the attachment to the nation) and patriotism (the attachment to the State) are hardly distinguishable and tend to merge. As contacts of this kind grow, the contrast with the politico-ethnic aliens, most of whom will be encountered in situations of conflict, will goad more and more of the State's population into an attitude of solidarity and cohesiveness, with the might and institutions of the State as rallying point. An exceptional degree of administrative malfunction, of material want, or of moral indignation with an existing regime, will be required in such a case to disturb from within the solidity of the State structure and to threaten either its integrity or even its basic stability.

An important and often-occurring deviation from this pattern should be mentioned here. It concerns the effect of more intensified contacts which go beyond trading and fighting and extend to social or intellectual consorting. Where the earlier forms of contact usually lead to xenophobia and to a heightened attachment to one's own nationality, an intensified form of social intercourse not infrequently leads to the blurring of national consciousness and to the arousal of links of solidarity with the corresponding elements across political and ethnic boundaries. This accounts for the familiar phenomenon of wide-spread familiarity and solidarity between rulers, aristocrats, large-scale traders, seamen, scholars, artists, diplomats and even professional soldiers of different countries, among whom—occasional wars and bitter competition and controversies notwithstanding—we find a certain *camaraderie*, a trans-ethnic and trans-State community of *mores* and intermarriage, even during periods when State and national rivalries were at their highest. The three best-known examples of this phenomenon are the hereditary European nobility from the Crusades on and till the present; the community of academic scholars beginning with the first universities and down to the replacement of Latin by the national languages as a vehicle of learned communication;[1] and the dynasties of Europe, whose interbreeding has reached such dimensions as to make them ethnically unidentifiable. These three strata are the first important cosmopolitan groups in the world. A deliberate attempt has been made since Marx to foster a similar cosmopolitanism among the class-conscious industrial proletariat. The attempt has not met with any substantial success, since the groups concerned don't enjoy much mobility and have little opportun-

1. The community of scholars has been somewhat disrupted after national languages have begun to displace Latin as medium of learning, but in the twentieth century we witness an organized attempt to re-establish it by fostering large-scale international co-operation and frequent meetings among scholars of different nations.

ity for actual intermingling. At most there is a certain softening of national antagonisms within its ranks due to indoctrination with the idea of class solidarity; and even that has not withstood very well the strain of war and other critical situations. Only among part of a thin upper stratum of politically active or highly educated labour leaders is there evidence of a *camaraderie* which tends to nullify ethnic distinctions, but then this stratum has become part of the fraternities of politicians and intellectuals, the modern equivalents of the rulers and scholars of old.

A different and very major problem confronts us when the ethnic unity is shattered *within* the State and contacts among the members of the various ethnic groups of the population, whether friendly or otherwise, are established within its boundaries. The situation may originate in several ways. One major avenue to it is conquest. The growth of most historic States has been a result of conquests, so much so that one sociological theory which used to be widely held and was highlighted by Franz Oppenheimer regards the very phenomenon of statehood as due to the establishment of the rule of a conquering group over another, conquered, one. When the conquering and the conquered groups belong to two distinct ethnic communities, the basic pattern of a poly-ethnic State is present. Within recent centuries, and down to our own times, dynastic arrangements, outright annexations and international treaties with or without preceding war have multiplied the instances of this pattern to such an extent that it fits most of the older States existing today. Another case is that in which the political community is not primarily based on the ethnic unity of its population at all, but on its religious unity or on dynastic allegiance—both very frequent phenomena down to the Middle Ages—or on a geographic grouping of a hetero-ethnic population (the cases of Switzerland and of the American republics) under circumstances in which ethnic and especially linguistic homogeneity is not initially regarded as particularly relevant to the political structure. Finally, there are cases in which a fairly homogeneous ethnic group, already living within a single State structure, experiences a process of differentiation under the influence of diverse alienating factors. In the past, appearance of religious heterodoxies served as the principal divisive factor of this kind; it is not impossible that lay ideologies of a socio-economic nature will play a similar role in the future.

In all these cases the poly-ethnic State has made its appearance, and the main issue is joined: how are the relations to be shaped between the two social phenomena—the State and the ethnic group—especially where the latter has reached that stage of self-consciousness, self-assertion and a more-than-local dimension which we designate with the name of nation—in conditions of non-congruence? In fact, these relations assume many different shapes. But at this juncture we consider the problem mainly from the point of view of those interested in the State. What perturbs them is that, given this non-congruence, the State can no longer rely for its cohesiveness on the double foundation of political allegiance and national-mindedness, on patriotism and nationalism. The cohesion of the State's population will be based now on one foundation—that of political allegiance, of patriotism—alone. The other factor—the ethnic one—will play, as far as members of non-dominant ethnic groups are concerned, the part of a disturbing element, and their very ethnic distinction, especially if it is raised to the level of national consciousness, will seriously reduce their identification with the State structure. Expressed in a formula, it can be said that while in the mono-ethnic State the intensity of cohesion is represented by the sum total of patriotism and nationalism, or $C = P + N$, in the poly-ethnic State the intensity of cohesion for all but the dominant ethnic group represents the difference between the two, or $C = P - N$. Where the pull of nationalism among the non-dominant groups is stronger than that of patriotism, the cohesion factor will be actually of a negative magnitude and will turn into a factor of disruption.

This being the case, the forces interested, for whatever reasons and for whatever purposes, in the preservation of the State will seek to devise means to that end. Quite obviously the monopoly or near-monopoly of superior armed force in the hands of the

State will prove a powerful weapon, likely under favourable circumstances to overcome disaffection on ethnical grounds for a long period of time, just as it is likely to overcome disaffection on any other grounds. This will especially be the case if there is nothing in the international situation that threatens the stability of the existing political regime or the integrity of the given State itself from the outside, and still more so if the State can count on some foreign factor that might actively support it against disaffective movements (the principle of legitimacy in the 1820s and 1830s; Russian intervention in Hungary, 1848). However, in the long run the State is interested in maintaining its hold over any considerable segments of the population not by force alone but also by intensifying their allegiance. Indeed, the more intense this allegiance, the less will the State have to rely on force, and the more certain it will be of their continued adherence even in the face of a serious crisis or of foreign threats. One of the most tried ways to achieve this end is to further the population's ethnic integration. This, if successful, will re-establish (or establish for the first time) the congruence of the political and the ethnic communities within the State's boundaries and will change the State into a mono-ethnic one. If this stage has been attained it does not mean that any other problems and shortcomings of organized society have been overcome. The State would still have to cope with economic troubles, social maladjustments, health problems, individual difficulties, ideological and power struggles, which habitually beset mankind; it would be freed from one specific set of troubles only—those that have their origin in inter-ethnic tension—but this is no mean alleviation. Only if this process of integration should prove, for some reason, impractical or undesirable, will the State leaders seek a solution based on a continued co-existence of several ethnic communities—in short, a solution on pluralist lines.

This division of the basic trends in dealing with problems of poly-ethnicity into an integrationist and a pluralistic pattern is merely a schematic way of dealing with the subject. In practice neither of the two patterns appears in pure form, and elements of either can be detected in each instance. We will see, however, that in every case the State leans more towards one or the other of the two trends.[1]

Over long stretches of time, integration seems to constitute the most plausible outcome of the co-habitation of several ethnic groups living in close proximity, especially when they live under common rule and where the territorial delimitation between their respective areas is incomplete. This is certainly the case when no special circumstances result in the placing of a particular value on the ethnic criterion as one that would be called upon to lend legitimacy to the political organization. If we look at the modern nation-States of Europe we shall see that, except perhaps for those of the Scandinavian peninsula, the population of each of them is largely the product of pre-existing ethnic groups which have integrated into the nations we know today. This is true of the French nation, consolidated from fairly heterogeneous elements between the seventh and the twelfth centuries. The English, despite several 'immigration waves', became a recognizable nation only a little later. Germans, Italians, Poles, Russians and Spaniards have all become the well-defined nations we know within a century or two of one another, though in the case of Russians and Spaniards, especially, a great many new elements were added later to the central core of the original national group. Medieval Europe furnishes us with a large number of well-authenticated 'melting-pots', and at the end of each and every melting process we find the identical phenomenon—a new integrated or composite nationality. Probably similar integration processes had gone on in other parts of the world and in earlier times, resulting in the formation of the Japanese, Chinese, Indian, Afghan, Persian, Assyrian, Babylonian, Jewish, Egyptian, Greek nations

1. In adopting this scheme we approach the nation-State relation from the point of view of the State. Were we to proceed from the point of view of the nation a different pattern would ensue: an 'integrationist' trend would be that which would lead towards the integration of all parts of the nation into one State *at the cost of existing States* (thus the unification of Germany and Italy in the nineteenth century and the movement towards the unification of Arab States at present), while a 'pluralist' trend would be one that accepts the division of the nation among many States, with all the attendant risks to national unity.

of ancient or medieval history, and of the nations of pre-Columbian Central and South America.

Under pre-modern conditions the process required a fairly long period of gestation. Our familiar expression of *melting-pot*—better yet, stewing-pot—illustrates the process very well. Put into the pot of physical proximity, covered by the lid of a common political system, exposed to the heat of cultural and social interchange, the various elements will change after a fairly long time—it took a few centuries in the past, but may take less in the future—into a brew. The brew will not be quite homogeneous. You can still point to a grain of rice, to a leaf of onion, to a chunk of meat, to a splinter of bone. But it will manifestly be *one* brew, with its distinct flavour and taste.

Similar processes continued and still continue to take place under more modern and under contemporary conditions. Here details of the process are observable and factors which make for its acceleration or slowing-down can be distinguished. The pressure of social contacts remains the principal catalyst of integration, and the greater social mobility of modern populations, as well as the greater penetrating power of modern mass-education and mass-communication media, both intensify and quicken this pressure. Of course, the same media, if put at the service of separatist, national ideologies, produce the opposite effect. We therefore often observe instances of integration and of counter-integrationist nationalism occurring side by side within the same society, thus leaving wide room for 'national self-determination' by the individual. A telling example during the nineteenth and early twentieth centuries is that of the Irish both in Ireland and in Great Britain: quite a number of them have integrated themselves with the British community, while others withstood integrating influences and developed an intense national consciousness of their own with far-reaching political effects. Another striking example is that of Jews during the same period, among whom we find both wide-spread 'assimilation', i.e. a tendency to integrate with the nationalities among whom they live, and a nationalism of their own, the latter leading again to the formation of an independent State. A similar pulling in both directions, with varying intensities, is found among Kurds in Iraq, among Scots and Welshmen in Britain, among groups of Slavic origin in pre-1914 Germany and Austria-Hungary, among various ethnic groups both in Tsarist Russia and the Soviet Union and among various ethnic groups in the Near East. Modern Asia and Africa, too, offer examples of both influences being active at once during the last stage of the colonial era and still more so in the newly independent States. However, what matters at this point is that in many a case it is integration that emerges as the prevalent result of a poly-ethnic population assembled within the same political structure.

The basic situation of poly-ethnicity, without which the problem of ethnic integration does not arise, is the rule rather than the exception today. The lesser mobility of past generations may have permitted mono-ethnic States to exist, and even that on condition that we choose to disregard certain significant differences. Japan from the middle of the seventeenth to the middle of the nineteenth century, disregarding the Ainu and a few other groups on outlying islands, came fairly near to being one. So were the sheikhdoms and principalities of inner Arabia, if we regard them as States and if we disregard the appearance of Jews, Persians, Negroes among them. So were, probably, a number of smaller States in Europe and elsewhere in the course of history, either originally—when these States represented tribal societies—or after a process of earlier integration had been successfully completed. But the essential mobility of the modern age, the vagaries of conquest and diplomacy, and the pervading march of international commerce, have made of the purely mono-ethnic State a thing of the past. Its last surviving examples—Saudi Arabia, the south and east Arabian principalities, the Himalayan States—have all succumbed within recent years, and today each of them experiences the impact of ethnically foreign elements. Poly-ethnic society has now become a universal fact.

The question that faces us is what the various forces active in the State are doing about this situation. The principal forces involved are the dominant ethnic group (in so far as there is one) or the ethnic groups so situated that they might conceivably compete for domination, the groups whose interests are centred on other than ethnic purposes (thus: certain, though not all, denominations; economic interest groups; class-conscious proletarians; groups united by non-economic interests and ideas), the formal governing institutions of the State, the secondary ethnic groups (mostly minorities, but sometimes numerical majorities), and the parties, leaders and spokesmen of all these.

A strong integrationist pull is exercised by the groups and individuals, other than those appearing on behalf of the formal State institutions, whose social interests are not primarily ethno-centric but rather inter-ethnic or an-ethnic. Without intervening too actively in the struggle, their very orientation will mostly tend to reduce the attention given to ethnic differences, to diminish the stress and tension resulting therefrom, and therefore their objective role will be that of an agent of integration. Where there exists in the State a dominant nationality such integration will mean, of course, the weakening first of the group-attachments, then of the group-awareness, and finally of the very group-identities and characteristics of the secondary ethnic groups, their gradual submergence within the dominant nationality, and the strengthening of the latter. This generalization must be applied with all due caution: if we say that such will be *mostly* the effect of the activities of clerics, class-conscious socialists, aristocrats, scholars, artists, economic interest groups, whose aspirations are not ethno-centric, we mean this and nothing more. There is no dearth of individuals belonging to these and similar groups whose aspirations *are* ethno-centric to a large extent. This is the case especially among intellectuals and artists of the so-called romantic school, some of whom have been among the most influential protagonists of national movements.[1]

1. We have already warned, however, against a shallow equating of romanticism with nationalism. While it may be true that a romantic in the sense of a non-rational, emotional element is present in each nationalist movement, not all romantic impulses are ethno-centric. Universalistic, religious, socialist, liberal and other movements are characterized no less by romantic impulses.

The groups that are most directly interested in a State-wide ethnic integration of the inhabitants are the groups personally connected with the State machinery in a dominant capacity; they will be found usually within certain strata of the dominant ethnic group which, more often than not, is pre-eminently represented in the machinery of the State. To them, successful integration means at once the strengthening of the State for whatever tasks may be set to it, the strengthening of their own national group and the increase of their own importance within the scheme of things. Viewed from the vantage-point of the leaders of the dominant nation, who are often identical with the leaders of the State, all these objectives converge, nationalism becomes identical with patriotism, and the destiny of the nation with the *raison d'état*. Such was and still is the attitude in Italy towards the small German and Slav minorities that lived or still live within her borders. Such was the case in pre-1918 Germany, where Germany's leaders aimed at the Germanization of the Slav, Danish and Alsatian and Lotharingian minorities. Such was also the Russification policy indulged in, though with less consistency, towards the non-Russian minorities in Imperial Russia. In this instance, oddly enough, this policy was shared also by that influential part of the ruling group which consisted of Germans; the 'reason of State' proved in their case a weightier consideration than their own group-identity.

Less direct is the integrationist policy adopted by policy-makers of the State in those countries in which the weight of the various composing nationalities is more evenly distributed and the chances of a successful assimilation of secondary nationalities to one particular nation appear more hazardous. In such cases the leaders of the State seek sometimes to strengthen the State's cohesiveness by minimizing the importance and the attraction of national values altogether and by focusing attention on a State-centred as distinct from a national-centred orientation. This, by and large, was the attitude assumed by the leading statesmen of the Austrian Empire during the century from 1815 to 1914 and, before the 1867 compromise, in Hungary as well. For a while statesmen of the Ottoman

Empire tried the same method. At the present time this is the main tendency of most leading statesmen in Latin America and in the poly-ethnic States of Africa and Asia. Whether or not the motto of nationalism is used, in fact they seek to transfer the weight of the principal ideological value from the ethnic group to the State. In a way, both these concepts, though based on social realities, are myths capable of cultivation and of denigration. What we find here is an attempt to cultivate the myth of the State at the expense of the myth of the nation.

In most cases State authorities are unwilling to leave integration entirely to the hazards of the unorganized pressure of social contacts, but embark on a deliberate policy of furthering integration by the means at their disposal. This is done in order to put more cohesion into the State structure by 'homogenizing' the population and discouraging the appearance of potentially deviant national movements. Such a policy characterizes to a greater or smaller extent all Western Europe with the exception of Belgium and Switzerland, all the countries in the Americas except Canada, all the Near and Middle East except Cyprus, Israel and the Lebanon, as well as Australia, New Zealand and most of the new States of Africa and Asia. Its nuances are manifold. It may consist in nothing more than a single official language and a tuition-free uni-lingual school system planned to serve as unifying media and accompanied by indirectly applied incentives calculated to favour integration, but without formal sanctions or official discrimination against members of non-integrated groups. This rather mild and liberal pattern is in use over most of Western and Central Europe and the Americas. In the United States its pursuit is known under the name of Americanization; in the other countries practising the system it bears no special name and a large part of the community is not even aware that it exists, which makes it no less real or effective.

The general characteristic of the system is an official policy favouring equal rights of individuals, whatever their ethnic origin, but discouraging or viewing as somewhat abnormal any claim of non-dominant ethnic groups to group-rights. This policy of furthering integration on the basis of individual equality while denying ethnic group-rights was a definite mark of Western thought and civilization during the age of Enlightenment. It remained strong throughout the nineteenth century, though towards the end of that period there began to grow, in competition with it, the idea that non-dominant ethnic groups, even when not destined to form States of their own, should benefit from collective rights as well as from individual equality. During the period between the two world wars the latter doctrine, though applied in practice to East-Central Europe only, gained wider acceptance in thought and literature in the shape of the 'protection of minorities' system. National pluralism within the State has thus gained a step on the age-old integrationist trend. However, that very period has demonstrated in several cases that the granting of collective rights to non-dominant nationalities does not necessarily induce in the latter a sentiment of satisfaction and growing loyalty to the State, after the example of Switzerland or even of Canada. In the countries of East-Central Europe it was seen that such collective status, put to use mainly in order to further the national self-consciousness of the minorities, merely stood in the way of their integration with the dominant nation without increasing their attachment to the State. On the whole, therefore, the State suffered a loss of cohesiveness which might become dangerous in times of crisis and gained no compensating advantage. Still more frightening to State patriots and to nationalists of the State's dominant nationality was the lesson of the Ukrainians in the south-east of Poland, the Hungarians in Transylvania and parts of Slovakia, and especially that of the Germans in the north-west of Bohemia, also known as Sudetenland. Here were national minority groups living in relative territorial concentration near the borders of ethnically kindred States, and in these circumstances the constant furthering of their national identities only contributed to their alienation from the State to which they were politically bound, and to their longing to be reunited with the ethnic kin across the frontier. As a result, though much of the pattern has been retained in the Soviet Union, in Finland, in Yugoslavia and a few other States of the region and has been adopted in Cyprus, Israel and the Lebanon, on the whole it enjoys today much less general favour than in the twenties and thirties of the century. Contemporary liberal thought demands an equal status for the individual regardless of his ethnic roots and links, but is much less insistent on the rights of the ethnic group as such, and where such rights are granted—whether in a liberal or in a near-totalitarian society—they are accorded more for reasons of convenience than because of considerations of principle. Internationally, too, the emphasis has shifted. The international community is quick nowadays to acknowledge the claim of a nationality that seeks to secede and to found a State of its own, and in this respect accords priority to the principle of self-determination over that of State integrity;[1] but, certain provisions of the Universal Declaration of Human Rights notwithstanding, it does not show particular concern for the preservation of national values of non-dominant nationalities *within* a given State. The integrationist pattern is prevalent once more.[2]

It does not detract from the essence of the integrationist pattern that in many a country it is applied in a liberal, relaxed manner and is compatible with a tolerant attitude towards the organized use of other than the official language, or towards the furtherance of some other hetero-ethnic features. Where the political regime of a State is generally strict, insists on con-

1. This rule is also not without its exceptions, as witness the attitude of the international community in the question of Katanga. The motivations in this case are of a political nature.

2. It should be noted that even in pluralist States the pluralist solution is applied only partially, in relation to a restricted number of nationalities which enjoy special rights. Thus, in Belgium—the French-speaking and the Flemish-speaking groups; in Canada—the English-speaking and the French-speaking; in Cyprus—the Greeks and the Turks; in Finland—the Finns and the Swedes; among the white inhabitants of South Africa—the English and the Afrikaners; in the Soviet Union—those nationalities and in those regions where a special status is granted; in Switzerland—the three (or four) constituent language groups. Individuals and smaller groups belonging to nationalities other than those specified are expected and encouraged to integrate with one or another of the 'acknowledged' nationalities.

formism or tends towards the totalitarian, there is often an attitude of intolerance towards hetero-ethnic manifestations even when they occur on a modest scale and present no conceivable danger to the cohesiveness of the overwhelming mass of the State's population. Where we encounter a very young national State, whose leaders are still so taken up with the newly discovered joys of sovereignty and, perhaps, do not feel yet quite secure about the solidity of their national cohesion, we are apt to encounter a similarly intolerant attitude, which is moderated, however, by considerations of opportunism or necessity. But where neither condition obtains there is apt to develop a wide measure of tolerance for foreign-language and minority-language schools in which children of citizens, and not only children of resident foreigners, are allowed to enroll, and foreign as well as minority languages are used in courts of law and in official documents within the country, without fear that the 'national' character or dignity of the State would be offended thereby. As long as these features present no tangible danger to the prevailing ethnic *status quo*, State authorities seem once more to be guided in these matters by the maxim of *de minimis non curat praetor.* Just as, for all practical purposes, we found it possible to consider as a mono-ethnic State one whose hetero-ethnic elements are a negligible component, so we may be allowed to regard those States as applying an integrationist policy, in which pluralist manifestations are held down to a minimum.

In contrast to that integrationist policy which is based on individual equality and on more or less indirect inducements, stands out the other variant of this policy which resorts to stronger measures, definitely discriminatory in character, in order to produce the same result. Here, too, inducements to integrate may be offered to hetero-ethnic residents by the dominant nationality and by the political authorities issuing from it; but side by side with them, sanctions are applied to those who refuse to integrate or are slow in integrating; so that the proverbial carrot-and-stick policy is carried on simultaneously and individual equality finds itself more or less seriously jeopardized. Policies of discrimination are not always integrationist in purpose. Nationalist or religious or racial in origin, xenophobic in sentiment, their purpose may be to maintain and strengthen ethnic distinctions, albeit on the basis of inequality, rather than to work towards integration. This trend, as practised in different countries and of which enforced racial segregation is an outstanding and wide-spread example, lies outside the scope of the present chapter. What we are concerned with at this point is discrimination as a means of pressure towards integration.

The use of this method was especially frequent in the service of a dominant religion. Beginning with antiquity, through the European Middle Ages and down to modern times, discriminatory treatment of adherents of other than the dominant religion was often used knowingly by State authorities as an aid in the dissidents' religious integration. The average Western reader may ask himself at this point what was the connection between religious conversion and ethnic integration. He should be reminded, therefore, that wherever the religious factor plays a major part in forming or continually linking ethnic groups—which is the case in all religiously oriented cultures, notably in pre-modern India, among Jews, in Byzantium, in medieval Spain, and among the Irish and Poles of the nineteenth century—religious integration or separateness is a decisive step towards ethnic integration or separateness. In the former Russian Empire, too, conversion to Greek Orthodoxy was a way to shed the disqualifications which, in varying degrees, accompanied membership in other denominations; and once having joined the Greek Orthodox Church an individual had his way smoothed into the Russian ethnic community.

More directly, in a number of countries knowledge of the country's official language, i.e. the language of its dominant nationality, is a formal condition for enjoying to the full the rights and opportunities which an individual might strive for in the circumstances. An elementary example is the practice, often encountered, of making the knowledge of that language a condition for granting citizenship status to adult alien residents. Another example is offered by the position which was held by the *évolués* in the African and Asian colonies of France during the last decades of the French colonial empire, and by similar native élites in Spanish and Portuguese colonies. What this amounted to was that these Powers encouraged the cultural integration of native élites, with a degree of equality as the prize for achievement, while practising stringent discrimination upon those who failed to make the grade. It seems, in parentheses, that this policy was started by the colonial Powers in question too late and—due to the social, economic and racially motivated opposition of the white settlers—was pursued with insufficient vigour, thus losing the race against incipient native nationalism.

The example just mentioned, of the only half-hearted manner in which the integration of the colonial population was pursued in the Spanish, Portuguese and larger French colonies,[1] sheds a light on an aspect of the situation which acts as a counter-influence to integration. Quite often the status of political pre-eminence achieved by a nationality in a given State goes hand-in-hand with a position of social pre-eminence and economic privilege far above that held by other nationalities or ethnic groups living there.[2] Such privileged position, whether it has developed as a result of political domination, has been the basis on which political domination grew, or has evolved side by side with it, requires the continued contrasting presence of underprivileged groups and, indeed, needs their presence as a pre-condition without which the existing situation may not continue. Integration, coupled with instantaneous or gradual equality, is apt to destroy that pattern of inequality upon which the position of the dominant nation rests, and this considera-tion alone may cancel, or at any rate slow down, the integra-

1. This does not apply to the smaller French island possessions in the West Indies, like Martinique and Guadeloupe, where integration was allowed to proceed rapidly and on a large scale. As a result, even the shock of French defeat in 1940 did not endanger those territories' attachment to France.

2. This remark is worded cautiously because exceptions are known to exist. Both in Eastern Europe during the inter-wars period and in Africa and Asia today situations exist where political pre-eminence and socio-economic pre-eminence are accorded to different ethnic groups.

tionist drive, however much the desire to preserve the State's integrity and to strengthen its cohesiveness may push the leaders of the dominant nationality in that direction. The history of colonialism is not the only one to provide us with object lessons of the workings and implications of this attitude. The attitude of large groups in the southern part of the United States of America towards Negroes offers another example of the kind. Further examples, sometimes equally radical, sometimes more moderate and hesitant, can be found in the history of the attitude of the leading nationalities of the historical empires of continental Europe and of Asia towards their 'subject peoples'. The extreme example, of course, is provided by the Nazi attitude towards Jews. In all these cases an exclusivist brand of nationalism develops within the dominant nationality of a State and finds its rationalization in a multitude of racialist, ideological or culture-bound conceptions, all purporting to justify the institutionalized superiority of the dominant nationality by its innate superiority. The price paid for this attitude is frequently the strengthened alienation of the non-dominant ethnic groups from the State and the arousal in them of a fierce nationalism of their own; but it is a price which the privileged nationality is sometimes willing to pay for the exclusiveness of its privileges.

Nevertheless, in many cases the impulse to strengthen the State by a purposeful furthering of the integration of its ethnic groups will prevail among the politically active élite over the exclusivist tendencies and will be carried out with reference to all or part of its ethnically heterogeneous inhabitants. The aim in these cases will be to make the hetero-ethnic elements feel themselves at one with the State ethnically as well as politically and at law. In other words: unless the political leaders of the State are willing to risk that ethnic groups will finish by changing and moulding State frontiers according to the shape of these groups, they will be driven to attempt moulding ethnic groups according to the shape of existing State boundaries.

It is a mistake, then, however commonly held, to believe that integrationist trends are basically inimical to all nationalism.

This is not so. An integrationist trend is merely a trend which results in, or seeks to achieve, the weakening and ultimate abolition of a set of pre-existing ethnic distinctions, and of the corresponding group-consciousnesses, only to be replaced by a gradually emerging inclusive ethnic group with its attendant group-consciousness. This emerging group will be based on a political community from the very beginning and its political significance will be stressed in all circumstances; therefore it will be a nation. What's more, self-awareness and self-assertion in the political arena will be inevitable under the circumstances; therefore, they will promote nationalism. A question that cannot be answered always in the same vein is whether the nation that will issue from the integration process will be essentially a continuation of the previously dominant nation with but secondary influences and features derived from the other groups, or whether it will be so different from any and all of its constituent elements that it may be described as a new nation altogether. The gradations will be many, and there will always be something arbitrary in the line of demarcation between an 'old' nation (e.g. the Greek or Jewish or Turkish nation) which has merely absorbed hetero-ethnic elements, and a new and composite nation (e.g. the Italian or Spanish or French nation). But in either case the end-product of a process of integration was never, as far as past human experience goes, a de-nationalized cosmopolitan society. At the end of the process of integration there was always the same kind of product: a nation.

Having depicted earlier some historical integration processes out of which have come the principal European nations known to us today, and having mentioned in passing the small-scale integration processes that have resulted in the continued absorption in these nations of hetero-ethnic splinter groups in more recent times and still do so, it may be useful to draw attention once more to the exact significance of the largest integration laboratories of our days—the countries of the American continent. Brazil is generally reputed to be the outstanding example of successful inter-ethnic integration, including inter-colour integration, existing today. Several recent studies have thrown light on this development.[1] They describe Brazil's success as due, among other circumstances, to a large-scale physical intermingling of races (*métissage*) in the past, to a timely stoppage of Negro immigration followed by a rapid tide of immigrants from a number of European countries, to an overwhelming unity of religion and language among all but the most primitive inhabitants of the country, to the traditionally 'liberal' attitude of the dominant strains[2] coupled with the 'docility' of Negroes and other non-dominant groups. There is one group, the Japanese—some 300,000 of them in a population of some 60,000,000—which seemingly does not integrate as yet, but this group, too, has not given birth to any grave tensions; one would expect that they too will be engulfed in the prevailing stream of integration.

It seems that the integrationist solution is also successful in the rest of Latin America, where general conditions are approximately similar. In many of the countries concerned the mixture of ethnic and colour strains is less diversified (notably in the Andean States, Argentina, Haiti, Mexico and Uruguay). Some minority groups work pretty hard at maintaining their group identities (Germans, Italians, Jews), and to some extent there is present an attitude of non-receptiveness of the principal ethnic groups towards some of the hetero-ethnic elements, especially so towards Jews: but the overall integrationist trend is clear. Organized pressure to integrate, by way of legal or social discrimination against unintegrated groups or of a compulsory educational pattern, plays but a minor role; the result is achieved mainly by the willingness of the secondary groups to integrate, and by the ready acceptance of them exhibited in most cases by the dominant linguistic-religious group. It is of interest that this trend prevails despite

1. In addition to the published studies available on the subject the author acknowledges gratefully the reports, not yet published, submitted to the 1961 Congress of the International Political Science Association by Professors Cavalcanti and Diegues, of the University of Rio de Janeiro.

2. Even the institution of slavery is said to have implied less of a social stigma and to have been handled more liberally in South America generally and in Brazil particularly than in the United States. Thus: S. Elkins, *Slavery*, 1959; F. Tannenbaum, *Citizen and Slave*, 1947.

the fairly pronounced difference in the economic and social status that exists between various ethnic, and especially between colour, groups—a situation which, by the standards both of Europe and of the Afro-Asian complex, might have been expected to lead to the intensification of inter-ethnic tensions and to their translation into the language of radical political claims. Such developments have indeed occurred in the past, and a few of the revolutionary upheavals in the area, especially that which took place in Mexico at the turn of the century, did have a distinct ethnic overtone. But of late this is no longer noticeable. Politico-ethnic claims seem to have lost their vitality in Latin America, and such political and social upheavals as have occurred in recent years bear no mark of inter-ethnic struggle.[1]

1. In so far as recent revolutionary upheavals in Latin America have a genuine ideological basis (which not all of them do possess), they have been labelled by their spokesmen as 'nationalist'. As used in Latin America with reference to conditions prevailing there, the term bears no ethnic connotation. It rather denotes a trend to complete the respective State's, and the entire region's, formal independence by a condition of greater freedom from foreign economic influence, especially from United States' influence. This trend manifests itself not only in revolutions but also in less violent developments. Foreign observers of the scene have adopted the term in the same sense. Thus: R. J. Alexander, 'Nationalism, Latin America's Ideology', in: *Journal of International Affairs*, vol. 15 (1961); and the March 1961 volume of the Annals of the American Academy of Political and Social Science: *Latin America's Nationalistic Revolutions*, especially the opening article by K. H. Silvert. This trend towards economic emancipation from foreign influence does not, of course, exhaust all the components of Latin American revolutionary upheavals. In the Fidelista revolution in Cuba, just as in the Mexican upheavals at the turn of the century and in the 1920s and in Argentina during the catering of the Peronista regime to the *descamicados*, there is the added element of a demand for a radical redistribution of wealth within the population for the benefit of the underprivileged strata.

Both the demand for freedom from *foreign* capitalist influence and that for redistribution of wealth within the population—at present very unequally distributed among the ethnic groups—may conceivably lead to the birth of an ethnically motivated exclusivist nationalism, such as we encounter in other parts of the world. A possible indication to that effect is the recent increase in Argentina and a number of other Latin American countries of anti-Jewish sentiment—habitually a sensitive barometer of

A somewhat similar pattern obtains in the United States of America as far as ethnic groups of European and Near Eastern origin are concerned. Theirs is the famous 'melting-pot' model of rapid integration into a single cultural group based on the English language as a medium of communication. Despite considerable influences of the secondary groups on the *mores* of American society, the imprint given to it by the earlier, mostly English-speaking, settlers prevails. Tensions among the groups, especially during the transitional, pre-integration stage, but also later on, are stronger than in Latin America, but in the long run the dominant group shows a fair measure of receptiveness to the absorption of others, and the process is aided by a considerable amount of physical inter-mingling. The one obvious difference is in the realm of religion: in this area pluralism is definitely admitted not only in law but also socially. In the case of Jews, with whom religion forms the very core of the ethnic identification, this circumstance exercises a retarding effect on the integration process. On the other hand, the tensions surrounding white-Negro relations in the United States are proverbial and form a distinct contrast with the situation in Latin America. If we add to that the difficulties placed by the dominant majority in the United States in the way of the full integration of Indians, Chinese, Japanese, Mexicans and lately Puerto-Ricans we may decide that the receptivity of the dominant English-speaking strain and of other groups stemming from Northern Europe to coloured strains, and even to nuances of colour, is far lower, and their 'allergy' to them far higher, than is the case among the inhabitants of the countries to the south of the United States. The explanation of this phenomenon is not a matter for the present study.

The over-all tentative conclusion offered here is that while integration works in Latin America as a well-nigh universal solution of possible inter-ethnic tensions, it resolves these

inter-ethnic tensions among the non-coloured peoples of the world. Up to the time of writing, however, Latin American nationalism so-called is not essentially a phenomenon of heightened ethnic self-awareness, such as forms the object of our preoccupation in this study.

tensions in the United States within the European and non-coloured complex only. For coloured groups individual equality is gradually being achieved in fact as well as in law, but a sense of ethnic heterogeneity is actively cultivated on the part of a sufficiently large segment of the dominant group to make their full integration a rather remote contingency. Because the coloured groups are relatively small when measured against the total population, the resulting tensions raise no serious political problems on a national scale that would not be capable of solution by trivial means.[1] In the more sensitive parts of the country, however, such as the Southern States, the New Mexico and Southern California area, the cities of New York, Chicago and Detroit, the ensuing political problems are serious indeed.

Canada is known to have adopted a bilingual system and therefore is justly regarded as tending towards ethnic pluralism. It should be emphasized, however, that the pluralist pattern applies to two communities only: the English-speaking and the French-speaking. As a matter of fact, wherever ethnic pluralism is applied it is always confined to certain qualifying ethnic groups; the other groups are expected to integrate with one of the privileged nationalities. This attitude is not unreasonable: pluralism *ad infinitum*, without regard to numbers, degree of territorial concentration and other factors, would be a practical absurdity. Where Canada is concerned this is an important point, for Canada continually attracts immigrants belonging to many linguistic and ethnic groups, and the policy towards them—as far as Europeans are concerned, at any rate—is no less integrationist than south of the border. There is both official and public expectation that these will integrate within, and assimilate themselves with, one of the officially fostered linguistic groups. The policy works reasonably well.

1. Such a trivial means of solving minor tensions is the practice of a judicious balancing of elective and appointive offices between members of different ethnic and colour groups. This means is resorted to quite openly in the United States, but in a more discreet form is practised in many a country either in lieu of minority group-rights or as supplement to the formal rights accorded to the ethnic or religious groups.

The position is more involved when it comes to the remnants of the original inhabitants—Indians and Eskimoes—and to the relatively few immigrant communities of non-European origin; but there, too, the beginning of an integration process can be discerned. On the religious side Canada, with its approximate balance between the two major Christian denominations, has accepted pluralism as determinedly as the United States, though on the basis of a different framework of State-Church relations.

On a smaller scale the United States type of integration is again encountered in Australia (with the added feature that non-white communities were drastically reduced or denied admission); the bilingual-plus-integration-of-others pattern of Canada substantially repeated in the manner in which the white part of the population is expected to behave in South Africa; and the relations between white settlers and Maori in New Zealand show something of that expansion of ethnic integration to the inter-racial field which has been noted in Latin America.

A question we may not evade is—where does all this integration lead us? We have seen that the older, already completed integration processes, about which we have learned in history and which we guess as having occurred in prehistoric times, have resulted in the crystallization of nations. A moment's consideration will show that in the contemporary laboratories of integration, in the melting-pots or pressure cookers of today, it is the same product that is being brewed. To take the best-known example, the mass of the population of the United States is rapidly assuming that character of relative homogeneity which marks a fully matured nationality. Whether that American nationality which is being born before our eyes will englobe all sections of the population or whether some or all of the marginal groups mentioned above will be kept at arm's length, sharing citizenship status but not becoming part and parcel of the new ethnic entity, is a problem apart, and certainly a very weighty one. But it does not affect the central fact. After having decried nationalities and nationalism as a European anachronism, America herself is becoming 'nationalized'. Nor is the nascent American nationality free from that heightened self-awareness, from that emphatic and emotion-laden concentration on its typical values (usually referred to as 'the American way of life'), from that insistence that the interests of the national community be made the major yard-stick of policy, which characterizes nationalism. Since the nascent nationality is certain to comprise the overwhelming majority of the population, the United States is about to become a nation-State such as we find in Britain, France, Spain, Italy, the Germanys and several smaller European countries. It is easily understood, therefore, that the conceptual distinction between the nation in the ethnic sense and the 'nation' in the sense of the sum total of the State's citizenry, just as in the cases of these European States, continues to be blurred in the mind of the average American; the more so since the United States has never gone through the phase of fighting the cause of the nation against a hetero-ethnic State. None the less, glimpses of a more exclusivist nationalism, with all its inherent excesses, have been appearing in the United States ever since the 'Know Nothing' movement and are certainly noticeable today, a nationalism in which the alleged values and interests of the dominant ethnic group were knowingly distinguished from those of the country as such. The more the marginal groups will be kept out of bounds of the nascent nationality, the more American nationalism will lift itself out of a more generalized, State-and-geography-oriented patriotism, and will come increasingly to resemble the nationalisms of the dominant nationalities of Eastern and Central Europe. The more the marginal groups will be permitted to integrate, the more nationalism and patriotism will tend to merge after the fashion of most of Western Europe. At present we encounter a self-styled American nationalism used ambiguously in both meanings, with the adjective 'national' applied more frequently to the politically circumscribed group of the inhabitants of the whole country (as distinct from the population of a single 'State' or region), and 'nationalist' to an ethnically determined group with exclusivist proclivities.

Still further progressed on the road to nationality formation is Australia, where the narrower range of the component strains has accelerated the process. However, the political and emotional links to Great Britain, the avoidance of friction with the mother country by the timely and ungrudging grant, first of dominion status and then of independence within the Commonwealth, and the relative paucity of groups upon whom an exclusivist attitude could be exercised, have all slowed down the evolution towards self-assertive nationalism. Even more than in the case of the United States the nation appears to the average Australian as identical with the whole of the country's population, and Australian nationalism, such as it is, is not yet distinguished from patriotism. What we have here is an almost completely formed nation-State, with a sense of kinship with some other nation-States with whom it shares a common language and cultural tradition, and with no irredentas or internal ethnic frictions to raise its ethnic as distinct from its political identity to the level of consciousness. Many observers, this writer included, will regard this condition an ideal one for any nation and will extend to Australia their wish that neither external nor internal complications may arise to disturb it.

A somewhat similar situation is shaping up in New Zealand except for the complication provided by the factor of European-Maori relations. This factor has slowed down the objective integration of the country's inhabitants into a single ethnic unit, has focused a certain amount of attention on the distinction between the ethnic and the political group, and may yet deflect the country from a predominantly integrationist to a partly pluralist pattern on a racial basis. Still more inclined towards a multi-national pattern reminiscent of many a European country is Canada. Disregarding the small marginal groups, the mass of the Canadian population is divided into two large blocs, of which one—the French-speaking—is exhibiting all the marks of a self-conscious and politically assertive nationality, while the other—the English-speaking one—is nearing that stage. Both nationalities are, of course, composite products of an integration process which is continually being nourished by immigrants of various origins who find themselves absorbed into the one or the other nationality. The very presence of the two major entities within one country gives rise to inter-ethnic tension which is typical for the multi-national States of Europe and which makes it impossible to ignore the distinction between the community of citizens and the national group, to confuse the State and its over-all population with the nation. At that, the reasonable manner in which these tensions are being resolved, and the territorial distribution of the major national groups, somewhat reminiscent on a larger scale of the territorial distribution of ethnic groups in Switzerland, offer a serious chance that the worst of the tensions may be allayed and the nationalities find satisfaction in their co-existence pending—perhaps—still fuller integration in the more distant future.

In South Africa, too, the inhabitants of European origin are divided into what an outside observer will regard as two major national groups. One of them—the Afrikaners—clearly designates itself as such, and the terminology of nationality and nationalism is fully employed by its spokesmen with all its familiar ethnic connotations. It is openly self-assertive, and in the defence of its values and interests it takes an aggressive attitude both vis-à-vis other white groups and, still more so, vis-à-vis the non-white population. The English-speaking group has a far less clearly defined ideology (a factor which many a reader will feel inclined to explain by reference to the alleged English dislike for theorizing and the preference for 'muddling through' by trial and error). Too weak to stand on its own feet, it liked to consider itself part and parcel of the British nation; but at a time when Britain—both as an Imperial Power and as a nation that used to send out settlers to the corners of the earth—is withdrawing her outposts, this position is no longer tenable, and so no clear and conscious goal is visible beyond that of keeping as much of the *status quo* as possible. But the ethnic group, at the time of this writing, still persists, and since it both claims and exercises influence in politics, it may be regarded at least as a national splinter-group. Both groups are products of integration: within the limits of a fairly restrictive immigration policy both have absorbed a number of hetero-ethnic elements and still do so on a reduced scale. Here again, then, we witness the formation of at least one and perhaps two nationalities, the relations between which, in this instance, have been marked from the start by fierce competition for domination, a competition in which success went first to one, then to the other party, and which is barely held in check by pluralistic institutions. What overshadows the picture is, of course, the presence in the country of a huge non-white majority, itself ethnically divided, devoid of any political rights worth speaking of and subject to gross inequality in other respects as well. It is this background of a non-dominant majority, ethnically distinct from both white nationalities and beginning to acquire a nationalist ideology of its own, which lends a somewhat unrealistic air to the continued manœuvrings of the two minority nationalities. In the long run the future of both of them will be determined by the solution which will be given to the inter-racial problem.

The foregoing remark holds with even greater force of the less numerous groups of European settlers who have lived or are living still in other areas of the African continent, from North Africa to Mozambique, Southern Rhodesia and Angola; only there the inter-racial problem has already found its basic solution, and this has gone against the formerly dominant minorities. Starting severally with French, English, Spanish and Portuguese stock and language, absorbing various hetero-ethnic and even hetero-racial elements in the process, some of these groups of settlers—especially those of Algeria and Southern Rhodesia—reached such numbers and became so rooted in their African surroundings that, given more time, they might have developed into distinct ethnic groups of major political significance in the respective territories. However, the factors that made for the successful march of the native populations towards independence have progressed at a speedier rate and have put a stop to that development. At present the settlers have withdrawn or are withdrawing from the region; those that will remain will be too insignificant in numbers to be regarded as anything more than splinter-groups of nations that have their centres elsewhere. Their links with the outside world and their still superior socio-economic status may enable them to retain an ethnic identity of their own instead of becoming integrated with the majority group, as such identity was retained, indeed, for long stretches of time by Greeks, Italians and Jews in Egypt; as demographic basis for national movements they can no longer be taken into account.

An as yet fluid situation with reference to the future nationality map confronts us in the collection of melting-pots represented by Latin America. As noted before, the integration process works there better than in any other part of the modern world. Pluralism as a mode of life within the individual State seems there to be definitely out of fashion. But when it comes to visualizing the end-product likely to emerge from the process the issue is complicated by the presence in the area of well over twenty sovereignties, well over twenty mutually independent political structures. It is not the presently current brand of Latin American 'nationalism' so-called that is directly relevant to the issue. We have seen that this movement is more sensitive to economic dependence on factors from outside the area than to purely ethnic stresses.[1] What matters from our point of view is to know to what extent the nationality-crystallization process in Latin America is going to conform to existing State boundaries, thus resulting in a series of nation-States, and to what extent it is likely to depart from them. In the latter case we would end up in Latin America with an ethnic map that would clash with the political map—a situation that may lead to complications and aggravated tensions.

The simplest cases in this respect are those of miniature Haiti and of gigantic Brazil. Set apart by its French language,

1. Another important point, though not directly relevant here, is that while North American nationalism, because its bearers are socially as well as ethnically dominant, is conservative, the budding 'nationalism' of Latin America, even in its Peronista variant, tends to march or at least to play with the Left, because its bearers seek to break the existing social *status quo* in which others are dominant. This is a feature which Latin American 'nationalism' shares with the national movements of the 'oppressed nationalities' in the Old World.

Haiti may already be said to have crystallized a nationality of its own, so that whatever the other shortcomings of its regime at least the State-nation relationship is based there on complete identification. Similarly, the body-politic of Brazil, set apart by its Portuguese linguistic and cultural basis, may easily pursue the well-advanced process of ethnic integration to the point of becoming one of the great nation-States in history. This, indeed, seems the more likely outcome; nevertheless, caution is advised: the country's vast expanses, the diversity of economic interests between its various regions, and the variety of the demographic composition of its population, may yet provoke both major ethnic differentiation and secessionist moves. Of the Spanish-language countries, the larger political entities such as Mexico and Argentina, Chile and Peru, as well as the smaller but sea-bound Cuba, represent each a mass sufficient to attract and mould their respective population into the shape of a distinct nationality: and with the assistance of the very real differences in the ethnic make-up of the populations concerned, the process is well on its way. On the other hand, there is a very real sense of both cultural and political solidarity among the intellectually active élites in these countries, coupled with a low sensitivity to the differences between the countries and with a high sensitivity to influences originating outside the area. It is not excluded, therefore, that Spanish-speaking Latin Americans may yet come to regard themselves as belonging to one large ethnic community. Should this come to pass it is also possible, though not inevitable, that the division of that community into several sovereignties may appear to them an anomaly, somewhat on the lines of the attitude that was taken by a considerable portion of the politically active parts of the German and Italian peoples prior to those countries' unification or by parts of the politically active groups in the Arab States of today. Doubts on this score are even more legitimate when it comes to the smaller States of Spanish Latin America, in which it may be seriously questioned whether each single State is at all likely to develop an ethnic identity sufficiently distinct from that of its neighbour or neighbours. Will there develop a Honduran nationality ethnically distinct from a Nicaraguan nationality? Or even a Bolivian as distinct from a Paraguayan, and a Colombian as distinct from an Ecuadorean nation? If not, will not the underlying ethnic similarities, assisted by the aggregative tendencies of modern life, render in time some of the sovereignties so artificial and redundant that they will be easily absorbed into larger political structures? In other words, what we may face is a repetition, *mutatis mutandis*, of what we have witnessed in Europe, *viz.* that in the long run it will be either the States that will succeed in forming the mass of their populations into single nationalities, or, failing that, the nationalities will re-shape the States of the area according to their image.

There is another, rather hopeful, feature of the Latin American picture that should be noted at this point. Despite occasional clashes, the mutual relations of the States of Latin America, ever since they have reached independence, are characterized by much less aggressiveness than was the case either among the nation-States or among the multi-national States of Europe. Should this characteristic continue into the future—so much the better. It may yet rob the entire problem of State-nation relations in Latin America of much of its explosive power, for in the absence of ethnic tensions and frustrations States may yet continue their existence on a basis no more rational than mere history-bred routine. There is no ineluctable natural law, after all, which postulates that a nation, either after crystallizing or after gaining independence, *must* seek aggressively to change the political *status quo*. That climate of relative moderation which has become typical in the early 1960s of many a State and of many a nationality in Western and Central Europe may just as well come to characterize relations in Latin America even after the process of nation-formation in that part of the world will have been completed.

What we see in Latin America is a spectacle of possible nationality-formation to which contemprary Europe offers no parallel, the development involved having taken place in Europe centuries ago: in addition to the struggle between integration and pluralism, within nations already existing, Latin America offers us an example of the earlier European process of integration and differentiation of inchoate nationalities. Pluralism within a given State doesn't seem to have much of a chance in Latin America, but the odds as between the integration of its peoples into one or a few Spanish-American nations and the growing differentiation of this as yet uncrystallized segment of mankind into a large number of nations paralleling political boundaries are as yet uncertain. In so large an area it is quite possible that both developments will occur side by side.

Another part of the world where a similar struggle between integration and differentiation is going on against a background of State-nation relations is that inhabited by Arab-speaking peoples. Here again pluralist solutions are rather frowned upon, and the attempts first of Assyrians and now of Kurds in Iraq, as well as of Druzes in Syria and the Lebanon or of Christian Copts in Egypt, to secure an acknowledged position as national minority meet with decided opposition on the part of the dominant ethnic groups. There is a similar disinclination to think in terms of ethnic pluralism in relation to Algeria, Libya and the Sudan, whose populations are by no means ethnically homogeneous. Pluralism on a religious basis is the most which is readily granted in the area, and even in this respect, except for the Lebanon, the pattern thought of is a pattern of factual inequality rather than of equality between the adherents of the dominant religion and those of minority religions. The decisive and as yet undecided rivalry in that region is between the trend towards a fuller ethnic integration of all or several Arabic-speaking peoples into one nationally conscious and politically assertive community, and the forces of differentiation. In many of the countries concerned the self-identification and the loyalties of a large part of the population still stop far beneath the level of the existing State, at the level of the village, the *hamula*, the tribe, the religious sect. In some cases the wider self-identification unit crosses State boundaries and pays but scant attention to them (thus in the cases of Druzes, Maronites and some not-yet-sedentary tribes both in Western Asia and in North Africa). This situation represents a serious source of weakness for the States involved, and hence it is the deliberate policy of the ruling élites to come to the aid of modern technology in undermining these parochial loyalties and in furthering State-wide integration and loyalty. At the same time, however, there is another movement afoot: that of furthering a consciousness of an all-Arab, or pan-Arab, nation, encompassing all territories in which the Arabic language is predominantly spoken, whatever the racial and other ethnic differences. This trend, supported by a large part of the Western-educated strata, and at times also by the rulers of the States involved,[1] if successful, would again threaten the existing State structure in the area, for it would tend to work towards their political unification on the German or the Italian model. Since the emotional grip of ethnicity is far stronger in this area than among the immigrant populations of Latin America, it does not stand to reason that the political map of the region could become stabilized without reference to the ethnic composition of its inhabitants.

In the long run, therefore, the ability of each independent State in the Arabic-speaking area to survive as such depends on its ability to accomplish a two-fold task: first, it would have to overcome the forces of objective and of emotive separatism within the large mass of its population and to foster the latter's integration to the point of objective and emotive unity; thereafter it would have to withstand the tendency towards integration and national consciousness within a still-wider pan-Arab framework, and to implant in its population the belief that the separate existence of the given State is justified by a real difference in the ethnic make-up of the population involved from that of the neighbours across the

1. The essential unity of all Arabic-speaking peoples is verbally affirmed by practically all governments involved, and their adherence to the Arab League in the face of serious political differences is a tribute to this attitude. If we analyse the record more closely we find, however, that the attitude of the rulers of a given Arab State to political unification of the area becomes more positive when it is likely to exercise hegemony and more negative when it is likely to remain a secondary component in the larger structure. This applies particularly to Saudi Arabia, Jordan and both the royal and republican regimes of Egypt and Iraq. It is less true of Syria, Yemen and the ruling élite of the Moslems in the Lebanon.

border. The former task is facilitated by the integrative forces, by proximity and mass-communications, and seems the easier to achieve, except where considerable non-Arabic-speaking groups are concentrated (Kurds; the tribes of Southern Sudan). Whether the second task can be achieved time will tell. It will spell the difference between a politically united or disunited Arab world.[1]

What, then, are the principal effects of the process of ethnic integration? They are of a two-fold nature. On the quantitative side the process results in the diminution of the number of separate ethnic groups. A political analyst, fearful lest a multitude of nationalities, each one a potential source of unrest in the political arena, may result in the 'balkanization' of the region, will be inclined to welcome this numerical reduction. So will the patriot of any given State welcome this process for its strengthening effect on the State (unless his particularistic or exclusivist nationalism exceeds his State-orientation). Similarly, a proponent of world unity might regard a diminution of the number of distinct nations as a basis for the reduction of the number of independent States and therefore as a condition facilitating the formation of a world State. On the other hand, the ethnologist or the romantically inclined folklorist might rather deplore the lessening variety in the rich tapestry of mankind, while any enthusiast of his own national group will deplore it should that nationality fall victim in the integration process, whatever his attitude to the process in other cases.

The second effect of the integration process is the premium it sets on the State—either the pre-existing or the newly-to-be-founded—as against the nation. Indeed, while now and then (especially in medieval Italy and Spain) we encounter nation-building integration processes going on irrespective of political frontiers, in most cases they manifest themselves within the confines of a single political structure and strengthen its

1. On the purely political level, and disregarding the ethnic problems involved, a federal or confederal formula, or even a league of States on the lines of the Arab League, can be adapted to either situation. But without a far-reaching measure of ethnic integration any such formula would offer but a precarious basis for a long-range arrangement.

cohesiveness by establishing the added bond of ethnic homogeneity.

Once the integration process has run a sufficient course the result will be, once again, a nation; and this nation, if confronted by stimuli which foster group-awareness and group-attachment, will once more exhibit the familiar phenomenon of nationalism. If the integrated nation has achieved independence within the framework of a mono-ethnic or a nation-State, this nationalism is further strengthened by becoming largely fused with the sentiment of political loyalty known as patriotism. The population of a nation-State is no less a nation, and is no less permeated with nationalism, because the nation itself is younger than the State, because the State has achieved independence in the relatively distant past, or because it denies the claims of other nationalities, which have not yet achieved similar status, to consideration in the political arena.

7

Pluralism on the basis of inequality

WHENEVER a politically organized society has failed to achieve ethnic integration it presents itself as a poly-ethnic or —to the extent to which ethnic groups have gained that importance as self-assertive factors in politics which stamps them as nations—as a multi-national society. This condition appears in a multitude of situations. It confronts us as a transitory phenomenon in a society or a segment of society which undergoes integration pending the completion of the process. In this case the condition is confined in its more serious aspects to a few generations and, beyond the admonition that sensibilities and interests be treated gingerly during that critical period lest severe inter-ethnic tensions develop and hinder the development of the process, need not further concern us. On the other hand, poly-ethnicity may appear as a condition in a State in which, for a variety of reasons, there is but little pressure for integration and the durable co-existence of distinct ethnic strains appears likely. When organized society, especially the State, has become reconciled to this condition and has made arrangements—formal or otherwise—to that effect, we deal with an ethnically pluralist society. Again attention should be called to the fact that the two currents of integrationism and of pluralism are not mutually exclusive, that they act simultaneously upon individuals and groups within the same society, albeit with unequal and changing effect, and that all we can do is to seek to establish which of them exercises the stronger influence in any given situation.

The historical and social contexts in which pluralist solutions predominate are extremely varied, and this variety is reflected in the many nuances of the pluralist solutions adopted. At this point let us consider those pluralist solutions which, rather than brought about by the desire of secondary nationalities to have their group-identities respected, are dictated by the desire of the ruling group within a dominant nationality, just as often supported or even stimulated by wide-spread feelings within the ranks of that nationality, to maintain the distinction between the ethnic groups, thereby obtaining a set of satisfactions for the dominant nationality and for its élite. Such satisfaction may be sought mainly in the direction of economic advantage, of political privilege, of social prestige, of high cultural standards, or in a combination of these. In every case the pattern pursued will be that of *pluralism on the basis of inequality*, the satisfaction achieved will be one of a *higher status* for the members of the dominant nation, and the specific method resorted to will be the method of *discrimination* practised formally or informally, in a milder or in a severer manner, upon the members of the respective secondary ethnic groups.

The presence of such a pattern does not imply the absence of social differentiation within the dominant nationality. It may well go hand-in-hand with a very marked stratification within that nationality, accompanied by very real sanctions of a social or even legal inequality as between its diverse strata. But even if this is so, or especially if this is so, there may arise a strong stimulus for members of the socially inferior strata within the dominant nation to assuage their frustrations by cultivating an attitude of superiority towards one or more of the secondary ethnic groups, while the socially superior strata of the dominant nationality may find it useful to stimulate this attitude for its value as a compensation for the inequality existing within the nationality. The spread of the attitude is only helped by the xenophobic, suspicion-of-the-stranger views which naturally are more often found among the less mobile and less educated strata than among their more sophisticated social superiors. Illustrations of this special xenophobic trend among the socially inferior strata of dominant nationalities abound throughout recorded history. Both in Eastern and Central Europe and in the southern part of the United States of America it is a well-known and abundantly studied phenomenon. Nor does the above exclude a dislike of hetero-ethnic secondary groups among the higher social strata of the dominant nationality. Only in their case, apart from causes connected with class-interests and with the psychological background of the individual, this attitude is linked with the generally exclusivist tendencies current within these strata. It is, in a way, an extension to members of a hetero-ethnic group of the disdain which these strata often exhibit towards their 'inferiors' of the same nationality, and is strengthened by the latter habit of mind.

Nor does the unequal pluralistic pattern necessarily imply a water-tight separation between the ethnic groups such as would make it impossible to move down or—what is more important—to move up from one group to the other. Societies which practise inequality and discrimination between ethnic groups are not always closed societies. Quite often we find them open to cross-ethnic mobility no less than to mobility across class and caste lines. Only, where in a prior context we have watched discrimination practised as a deliberate means to *induce* wide-spread integration, we find at this juncture discrimination used to preserve ethnic distinctions to the advantage of one nationality, with integration discouraged as a matter of principle and appearing in the role of a rather exceptional avenue of escape from inequality. It is quite possible, of course, that one part of the dominant nationality's élite may aim at integration in the interest of the State's cohesiveness, while another part of the élite, or a large part of the inferior strata, may consciously or unconsciously oppose integration. There are also cases on record in which integration is met with greater acceptance on the part of socially inferior strata than on the part of the more exclusivist-minded élite; this has notably been the case in Latin America.

The common denominator of all forms of inequality practised in the service of ethnic pluralism is that all of them are used to ensure or to strengthen the predominance of one ethnic group over the others. History, both ancient and recent, furnishes us with many variants of the pattern. A brand of inequality singularly revolting to the modern mind is that which, not content with discriminating against the group as such, places severe and exceptional burdens on the individual because of his ethnic links. Slavery on an ethnic basis was one of its best-known and extreme forms. It has survived officially until quite recently, and its traces are still found in isolated corners, sometimes in the alleviated form of peonage or bonded labour. Here the inequality is both socially effective and sanctioned by law. Another form of inequality often found is that which severely limits the freedom of sojourn, movement and occupation of secondary ethnic groups beyond those limitations which are generally practised in the given society.[1] An extreme instance of this kind, at the time of writing, is the regime of restrictions to which various categories of non-whites are subject in South Africa. Some of the occupational restrictions placed in Hindu traditional society on members of lower castes come under this heading, in so far as the division into castes carries ethnic overtones. Another example is the restriction placed in medieval Europe, and in Russia down to 1917, both on the area where Jews were permitted to live and on their range of occupations. Limitations of this kind are not necessarily anchored in law and formally sanctioned by the State. They may be based on less formal restraints and still prove quite effective. Cases in point are discrimination in selling and leasing dwellings to Jews, Negroes, Puerto-Ricans, West Indians and sometimes other ethnic groups either by private agreement or by silent consensus, as practised in

1. Less directly relevant to the issue are the restrictions, sometimes quite severe, to which certain ethnic groups are subjected in times of war or similar emergencies on grounds of security, such as the deportation of Volga Germans and of certain groups in the Baltic republics by the Soviet Union before and during the war with Germany, the deportation and special supervision of Japanese-Americans on the west coast of the United States during the war against Japan, and the special regime to which Arabs in the border areas of Israel are subject in the absence of normal relations between Israel and the Arab States.

certain localities in the United States, Britain and elsewhere, discrimination in employment as practised on an ethnic basis by employers in certain fields of economic enterprise, and the refusal of some 'white' trade unions to admit to membership or to acquiesce in the employment in the trade concerned of non-white labourers.

Disqualification for special occupations which carry a high social prestige, such as appointive or elective public office, is less onerous for the large mass of individuals belonging to the ethnic group, but striking, as it does, at the group's most articulate stratum, it is likely to arouse sensibilities to a high degree. This is also true of purely social discrimination, such as non-admission to clubs and associations with a high prestige-value: while it strikes at no appreciable economic interests or State-protected rights and involves concerns which might be considered trivial, this kind of discrimination touches the most dignity-conscious and status-sensitive strata of a secondary ethnic group at a point where sensibilities are most easily aroused.

Of special significance in a society in which the rudiments at least of democracy are valued, is a discriminatory treatment of members of a secondary ethnic group in respect of political rights. These are the rights through which the individual's position as an active citizen, with a voice in the affairs of the community, is manifested. Eligibility on an equal basis to public office, already mentioned before, is a case in point, and so—only affecting a much greater multitude—are the right and the opportunity, again on an equal basis, to vote at political elections and plebiscites. Just as in other instances of discrimination, inequality must not necessarily be expressed through the complete *denial* of the right or opportunity in question; it may also find expression in the right's or opportunity's partial curtailment, such as placing on the member of the secondary group of additional conditions for the exercise of the right or such as giving his vote—by manipulations of the electoral system or of electoral geography—a lesser weight compared to that of the vote of a citizen belonging to the dominant nationality. Here again, factual discrimination may be combined with legal discrimination or be substituted for it. Education is a further field particularly susceptible to ethnic discrimination. Total non-admission or a *numerus clausus* in the admission to certain schools or educational facilities, unequal distribution of manpower and budgetary means among schools likely to cater to members of different ethnic groups, and the consequent closing or restricting of certain opportunities to these groups, have been and remain fairly wide-spread practices.

Many of the restrictions here mentioned cut deeply into the 'equality of the individual before the law', which is presumed by the modern mind to constitute a basic prerequisite of civilized society. But of special importance from the legal point of view will be those forms of discrimination in which even the *access* of the individual to legal remedies, to courts of law and to the defence of his rights by other public authorities, will be less complete than that of his co-citizens on account of his ethnic links.

The extremes of inequality as a weapon of an exclusivist, anti-integrationist policy, slavery apart, are reached when steps are taken for the physical elimination of the ethnic group which forms the object of discrimination from the community. In ascending order of gravity these steps are (a) enforced segregation; (b) expulsion from the territory; and (c) extermination. Unfortunately, all three measures have been resorted to all too often in the course of history. Enforced segregation is an aggravated form of that restriction of sojourn and movement which has been commented upon already. A further step is the expulsion of hetero-ethnic elements from a country's territory. Here exclusivism runs the whole gamut of intensity and, rather than stopping at the stage of permitting or even forcing the secondary group affected to remain in the country while placing obstacles in the way of its integration, it seeks to eliminate it altogether. The purpose of this policy is no longer pluralistic; the policy aims rather to reduce the poly-ethnicity of the State, and were it practised towards all secondary groups it would render the State mono-ethnic. In a different and far more brutal way it achieves, if successful, the same end which is pursued by a policy of integration.

Expulsion on ethnic grounds is regarded on principle as abhorrent to the modern mind. Nevertheless, in certain specific circumstances the tensions likely to be aroused by a given poly-ethnic situation and the relief that may be expected from a determined move in the opposite direction are so palpable that some modified form of expulsion has been regarded as a tolerable means to that end. One kind of this modified expulsion is that practised in many a case of boundary changes. That part of the population involved which was unwilling to accept allegiance to the new sovereign was often compelled to leave the area. In most cases this process was neither compulsive in a formal sense (not for nothing has it been given the name of 'option', thus stressing the choice involved), nor directly linked to the ethnic group, but in fact the division of the population into those leaving and those remaining behind tended to coincide very largely with their ethnic self-identification, while a choice between so drastic a set of alternatives can hardly be distinguished from outright compulsion. But there is no lack of instances in which expulsion consequent upon territorial changes was both more openly compulsive and more directly linked with the ethnic identity of the expellees. Notable cases are the expulsion of the families of post-1871 inhabitants of Alsace-Lorraine upon the area's return to France in 1919 and the expulsion of Germans and Hungarians from territories that passed into Russian or Polish hands or that returned to Czech and Yugoslav rule after the Second World War. Not essentially different are the 'exchanges of populations' of either a compulsory or 'voluntary' character—the distinction between the two being semantic rather than real, since the 'voluntary' exchangee departs under the impact of pressures no less strident, often more strident, than those caused by legal compulsion. Exchanges of this kind were begun on a large scale between Bulgaria and Turkey and between Greece and Turkey after the First World War; after a lengthy period of social maladjustment and material suffering they have given the exchangees concerned a feeling of security and of belonging and have brought to an end a long-standing feud between countries and peoples.[1] The practice continued in a number of relatively little-known cases during the Second World War and beyond.[2] A further variation on the same theme is the series of more or less spontaneous movements of people, usually members of religious, racial or ethnic (in the narrow sense of the word) groups, who fled from their original domicile to another country in fear—whether well founded or not—of discrimination or persecution. Such movements, whether two-directional and therefore akin to 'population exchanges' (as between India and Pakistan, or between Israel and the Arab countries), or uni-directional (Armenians from Turkey, Frenchmen and Jews from Algeria), are, once more, 'voluntary' in a formal sense, but, because of the pressures involved, compulsive in fact. The attitude of outside observers in all such cases, unless coloured by specific political interests involved, will be largely determined by the conditions in which the uprooted groups are permitted to emigrate, by the opportunities offered to them to seek readjustment, and by the extent to which the process contributes to the settlement of international conflicts. The over-all meaning of the movements in question is, of course, the assertion of the interests of a State and of its territorial integrity over those of the secondary ethnic groups involved, and their over-all effect on the State concerned is in the direction of its greater ethnic cohesion.[3]

1. The classical studies of this movement are: S. P. Ladas, *The Exchange of Minorities*, 1932, and P. E. Moseley, *Repatriation of Greeks, Turks and Bulgars After the Greco-Turkish War*, 1941.

2. J. B. Schechtman, *European Population Transfers 1939–1945*, 1946.

3. A variant of the above is the deportation of a hetero-ethnic group from its traditional habitat in a given area within the State's territory to another and distant part of the same State. This policy is made use of in order to place members of an ethnic group under conditions which would render it more difficult for them to maintain their ethnic identity or, at any rate, would present less of a threat to the State's territorial integrity and strategic interests. The policy, one of great antiquity (it was assiduously cultivated, among others, by the ancient Assyrian Empire), has experienced a recent revival. As mentioned before, it was practised on a large scale by the Soviet Union on the Volga Germans, on part of the populations of the

A method complementary to expulsion of hetero-ethnic elements or to a policy which encourages their emigration is the total non-admission or a restrictive admission policy towards such elements. From a formal point of view the two methods seem very far apart; in the first contingency the problem is one of the treatment by a State of its own permanent residents, usually its own citizens to boot. According to traditional legal doctrine, the manner in which a State treats its subjects is, within fairly wide limits, its own affair. It is true that this doctrine is rapidly losing ground to a more generous view according to which the observance of reasonable minimum standards of behaviour towards them and a certain measure of equality in their treatment are both required by those modern legal standards with which each civilized State is expected to conform and placed under the—albeit imperfect—protection of the international community. But neither strict law nor prevailing standards of social conscience restrict as yet the privilege of the State to regulate or to deny entry to aliens on any terms it sees fit to impose. From the point of view of the over-all effect on the ethnic composition of a given State's population, non-admission or a restrictive admission policy is as effective a method of manipulating this composition as any other. And here again, just as in the cases of outright expulsion, compulsory exchange, and emigration under pressure, the final effect of the discriminatory treatment is to reduce poly-ethnicity within the State.

The third form of extreme discrimination is that of physical extermination. This is done either by officially tolerated or veiledly supported action of the populace (rather frequent in the Middle Ages towards religious nonconformists, more recently in the form of Jewish pogroms in the Ukraine in the seventeenth century and in 1918–19, Armenian and Greek massacres in Turkey at different times prior to recent decades, and Assyrian massacres in Iraq in the 1930s) or even by direct governmental action. Of the latter, the killing of millions of

Baltic republics, and elsewhere, in 1940 and during the following war years, and—albeit as a temporary war measure—by the United States of America on the west-coast Japanese-Americans in 1942.

Jews, Poles, Russians, gypsies and others on the orders of the German Government during the Nazi regime is the most recent and—coming as it does in an enlightened era at the hands of the government of a highly civilized people—the most execrable instance. The future will show whether the revulsion of feeling that has occurred after the event and the subsequent advocacy of measures against genocide will succeed in eliminating at least this form of barbarity.

In glancing over all these manifold varieties of inequality we should realize that none of them had as its object ethnic groups only. They are equally likely to be directed, and actually have been directed, at groups whose heterogeneity was in the main political, economic, social or ideological in character. Many a time they were directed against religious heterogeneity even where this had no ethnic connotation. But so deeply rooted and so widely spread is their use against ethnically heterogeneous groups in their various racial, linguistic and religious contexts that they may not be lost sight of in any exhaustive discussion of the State-nation relationship.

We have seen, in this and in the preceding chapter, that discrimination has been used both to further integration and to hinder it, both to ensure poly-ethnicity on an unequal basis and to eliminate hetero-ethnic elements. Further reflection will show that, as often as not, discrimination, rather than furthering the integration of secondary groups, tends to induce in them strong nationalist sentiments. Whether these will prevail against the weight of the State and of its dominant nationality depends on the respective strength of the rival forces as well as on external factors. But other things being equal, human experience has demonstrated that equality is a better solvent of ethnic identities, a better sedative for self-assertive nationalism, than inequality; and that the latter, its inhumanity aside, is a rather uncertain avenue either to integration or to the maintenance of one ethnic group's superiority over another.

8

Pluralism on the basis of equality

THE attachment of the members of a secondary ethnic group to their group individuality and to its outstanding myths and values often proves too strong, either because of environmental factors, or because of the pull of tradition, or because of intensive ideology and propaganda, to be shaken by egalitarian inducements to integration. External factors, especially those stemming from outside the State boundaries and connected with international politics, may whip up group-awareness and group-attachment among members of the secondary group to the point of rendering most of them immune to integrating influences. Still more questionable, as we have seen, are the results of a policy of discrimination undertaken as a means to induce secondary ethnic groups to integrate with a dominant nationality or to merge into one. When carried out with sufficient ruthlessness discrimination may *eliminate* secondary groups from a State's territory; but where this result is not achieved, the most likely over-all outcome under modern conditions, and despite numerous cases of individuals passing over to the ranks of the dominant nationality, is the strengthening of the self-awareness of the group discriminated against and the appearance among its ranks of an articulate demand for a change in the status of the group. Neither the carrot of individual equality, nor the stick of discrimination, nor the stick-and-carrot in combination, have proved a reliable method for ethnic integration where the over-all conditions favouring such a development were lacking.

Where such conditions are lacking, a sustained state of dissatisfaction with existing ethno-political arrangements in the poly-ethnic State is apt to develop among secondary ethnic groups, and it is the spokesmen for these groups who take the lead in demanding a change in the State-nation relationship. At its most modest their demands assume one of two forms. If the existing State structure denies individual equality to group-members, either so as to stimulate their integration or so as to keep them in a status of inferiority, spokesmen for the group will mostly insist on such equality without showing any inclination to forgo group-identity. If the State has granted individual equality in the expectation that it will lead to integration, spokesmen for the group begin to preach continued and intensified loyalty to the group without, of course, abandoning the individual equality already obtained. Since the ethnic group appears in both contingencies as a politically active and articulate factor dedicated to its own continuance, it can be said to press for a policy of ethnic pluralism, a pluralism on the basis of equality; and where the other forces in the State, driven either by principle or by necessity or by a combination of both, acquiesce in such a pattern, ethnic pluralism on the basis of individual equality becomes in fact the prevailing pattern of the State.

Informal pluralism

This first and modest expression of ethnic pluralism—a certain measure of group-identification which, in effect, expects little more than individual equality in law, equal opportunity in fact, freedom of association on their own terms for those group-members who prefer to cultivate their traditions, and a certain amount of recognition in political preferment—is easier to maintain in States of mass immigration and in those where the secondary ethnic groups are numerically and otherwise insignificant than in those States in which the secondary groups involved are both numerous and have deep historic roots. This is so because the secondary groups in question are too weak or are not sufficiently stimulated to demand for themselves a more significant role in the political set-up. For the same reason—because the groups are too weak to endanger the State's cohesiveness in the long run—the leaders of the State and the authoritative spokesmen for its dominant nationality can afford to accept this situation with a minimum of resistance or with no resistance at all. An equilibrium is thus created between a rudimentary group-awareness and group-solidarity on the part of the secondary group and its willingness to let itself be influenced by the non-compulsory integrationist influences which stem from common citizenship. When the State, or a significant portion of its dominant nationality, are not swayed by strong currents of integrationist or exclusivist nationalism, of religious or of racial intolerance, this equilibrium is fully acceptable to them too.

We find this pattern established in Latin America, to a large extent in the United States of America, in Britain, in France, in the Netherlands and in a number of similarly situated countries, where the historic process of integration seems to proceed smoothly in a fairly relaxed, liberal context. Together with a fair measure of individual equality regardless of ethnic distinctions, a little measure of voluntaristic ethnic pluralism is agreed there by all but a fanatical fringe of dominant-nationality nationalists precisely because only little pluralism is demanded, because that little is essentially voluntaristic and does not require formal adjustments of the State structure, and because of the valid expectation that whatever little pluralism there is will not hold its own against long-range integrationist forces.

A different picture is encountered when a secondary ethnic group, either because of its numbers and territorial concentration or owing to a nationalist ideology supported by a favourable international situation, or stimulated by discrimination, sets its aims higher. Now, the group's articulate spokesmen, with a significant mass movement behind them, demand a special status for the group that would ensure for it formal participation in the institutions of the State. Individual equality is still insisted upon, but this is merely part of a far more ambitious political programme. In other words, the secondary ethnic group becomes a nationality and the bearer of a national movement. The State in question is not only a poly-ethnic but also a multi-national State. It depends on the respective strengths of the dominant and of the secondary nationalities within this State, on the intensity with which the one is determined to resist the demands of the secondary nationalities and the other to enforce these demands, on the ideological currents prevailing at the time, and on the international situation, to what extent the secondary nationalities will succeed in bringing about structural and social changes in the State which hitherto had reflected mainly the interests and wishes of the dominant nationality.

Religious pluralism

The one form of pluralism which, ever since the era of enlightenment, has gained the widest acceptance, is religious pluralism. This was certainly not the case in former times, and some of mankind's best minds, from Plato to Rousseau, expressed serious misgivings about it. But in modern times its value is taken for granted to such an extent that deviations from the principle are regarded as anachronisms or as anomalies in need of special explanation. When adherence to a religious denomination is somehow linked to membership in an ethnic group the denomination is still accorded recognition as a body with a large measure of State-sanctioned self-government and with tools adequate for the performance of its essential functions. Not always does such recognition carry a status of equality with other religious bodies, and many are the countries—Britain,[1] Ireland, Italy, Spain, all Scandinavia, Greece, Ethiopia, Iran, Pakistan, Afghanistan, most of the Arab States and most of the countries of Latin America—in which, to this very day, there is an official or established Church which enjoys privileges, ranging from very important to rather trivial, denied to all other denominations. Then again there are countries in which a given religion exercises in fact strong influence over the State's legislation and policies even though it does not enjoy officially a privileged position.

1. More precisely England and Scotland, but not Wales with its system of disestablishment.

Thus India, Israel, some Latin American States and—in a way—the United States of America. But in any case the recognition accorded even to the secondary religions and even where they lack equal status suffices to enable the given religious groups to conduct their organized activities with a certain amount of State protection.[1] Quite often they enjoy today, and still more often they enjoyed in the past, ever since the end of the wars of religion, a far greater measure of equality than do or did their individual adherents in their individual capacities; and even where the latter are still seriously dissatisfied with their political or social status they, *qua* communicants of organized religious bodies, and the religious bodies themselves, may be quite content with their station. This is so even in cases where the ethnic group and the religious group are directly linked and virtually identical in composition.

The above summary should not mislead us into thinking that the relationship of State and religions is otherwise shaped according to a uniform pattern. The contrary is true. In some cases the relation between the secondary denominations, or between all religious denominations, and the State is based on their treatment as public bodies entitled to support, even financial support, by the State (Belgium, Ireland, Israel) or

1. Few are the countries today in which religious pluralism is frowned upon to the point of seriously hindering the free exercise of non-dominant religions. Saudi Arabia and, at a distance, Spain are the principal surviving instances, with a few Latin American countries following in their wake. But in these countries, too, the tendency is towards relaxing the attitude in favour of more pluralism. Finally, there are some countries—Mexico in the 1920s and most communist countries today—which, while allowing and even formally stipulating religious pluralism, regard any religious creed as a possible rival of the State for the inhabitants' allegiance and therefore discourage the exercise of all of them. In practice, equality of treatment is no more observed in these cases than where the State favours religion or is neutral towards it. Depending on the interests involved, a State distrustful of religion may centre its disapproval on either the prevailing denomination (Mexico at the time indicated, Republican Spain in the 1930s, France at the turn of the present century, the Soviet Union in its early years) or on one or more of the secondary denominations (Soviet Union beginning with the 1930s, Yugoslavia in the late 1940s).

entitled to tax their members (Germany under the Weimar Republic); in other cases the relationship is based on the theory of separation of State and Church under which all denominations are regarded as the private concern of the communicants (France, United States of America, the countries of Eastern Europe); and then again there are countries with a mixed system under which one or a few religions are granted public status while others are treated as more or less private associations (United Kingdom, Sweden, Canada). Aside from these formal attitudes there is the informal but highly significant distinction between countries in which prevailing social attitudes favour religious affiliation and regard it as a socially beneficial phenomenon (Western Europe, most of America), countries in which dominant opinion looks upon religious affiliation with disfavour (communist-dominated countries), and those which hover between the two approaches. The details of these distinctions do not concern us directly, since they bear no special relation to the ethnic problem. It will suffice to state that under modern conditions the closer the connection between religious groups within a State and its ethnic groups and the more the two tend to coincide, the more often we shall find evidence of religious tension. This reciprocal intensification of religious and national tensions resulting from close links between the two groups is illustrated, for the recent past, by the Catholic-Protestant tension in Canada and Ireland, by the anti-Catholic mood in the United States at the time of Italian and Irish mass immigration, by the orthodox-heterodox tension in Tsarist Russia, and, for the present, by the equivocal position in which the Jewish community often finds itself. In other words, where religion is linked with a specific ethnic group the fate of religious pluralism tends to be influenced by the terms on which the ethnic groups settle their co-existence.

Linguistic pluralism

A second area in which pluralism is often exercised is that of languages. Where more than one ethnic group inhabit a State it is usual that each of them speaks, and in practically all more or less civilized communities writes, a language distinct from the others. Not for nothing is the language habitually spoken, or the 'mother language',[1] regarded as of such cardinal importance in the marking of identifiable ethnic groups that superficial observers tend to make linguistic distinctiveness the one decisive evidence of ethnic distinctiveness. This, as we shall presently see, is not quite correct, but it is true that an ethnic group being in the main one in which intense social communication has produced a community of *mores*,[2] a common language, representing as it does a prime vehicle of communication, plays a preponderant role. Though at a later stage, once the ethnic pattern has been set, this part may diminish, during the formative period of the ethnic group a common language is indeed indispensable. The following reservations will explain why a complete identification of a linguistic with an ethnic group must nevertheless be ruled out.

(a) The fact that two groups of human beings, located in *different* States, speak the same language does not necessarily stamp them as belonging to the same ethnic group. English is the predominant language in Great Britain, in Ireland, in the United States of America, in Australia, among the educated strata in Liberia and to a large extent among similar strata in a wide range of countries from the west coast of Africa to the Hawaii Islands. This does not entitle us to conclude without further investigation that all of these belong to the same ethnic group, while further investigation will disprove the idea still more. Similar conclusions will have to be reached with regard to the French-speaking inhabitants of France, Belgium, Switzerland, Canada, Haiti and the modernized strata in the former French possessions in Africa and East Asia; to the Portuguese-speaking inhabitants of Portugal and Brazil, and to the Spanish-speaking inhabitants of Spain, most Latin American republics, Puerto Rico and the Philippines.

1. The two need not necessarily coincide, though they do so mostly.
2. The point has been especially emphasized in K. W. Deutsch's *Nationalism and Social Communication*, 1953.

(b) Even within the same State it may not be taken for granted that all those who speak the same language constitute a single ethnic group. The point is obvious when we think of the English-speaking American Negro and of the educated native strata in the colonial areas at the time when these were still included within the political structures of the British, French, Spanish and other colonial empires. But it is equally true of the English-speaking Irishmen prior to the independence of Ireland and, by and large, of the Arabic-, English-, French-, German-, Italian-, Kurdish-, Persian-, Polish- and Russian-speaking Jews of many a country; whether or not these are considered a nationality, they will be pre-eminently regarded by themselves and by others as a distinct ethnic group.

(c) Just as there is no objective criterion of the minimum kind or range of distinctiveness which makes for a distinguishable ethnic unit, so also there is no objective criterion of the minimum linguistic difference necessary to conclude at the existence of a distinct language. In both cases prevailing attitudes and values, rather than objective differences, will determine the conclusion. In the case of languages we may find that phonetically and philologically the distinction between Yorkshire English and Cornwall English, between Platt-German and Austro-Bavarian German, between Provençal, Auvergnat and Brabant French, between Calabrese and Piedmontese Italian, is no smaller than that between Serbo-Croatian and Slovenian, between Bulgarian and Macedonian, between Latvian and Lithuanian, between Russian and Ukrainian, between Polish and Czech, between Swedish and Norwegian, between Dutch and Frisian, and yet the former are regarded by the communities in question as mere dialects to which no or none but folkloristic significance should be ascribed, while the latter are valued by their respective speakers as distinct languages and as a possible basis for asserting ethnic distinctiveness and political claims.

(d) Finally, even where linguistic differences are so pronounced that the extreme difficulty of verbal or written communication between two groups is beyond doubt, such groups may still—especially when living within the same political structure—show such similarity in their mode of living, in their inherited ideas, or at least in their striving for a common future, that they, and outside observers too, will regard them as forming for all essential purposes a single ethnic unit or, at the very least, a single though composite nationality. We find this situation to be true of different provinces in China, of several areas in India, in the relationship of Alsatians to the rest of Frenchmen, among some of the groups generally regarded as belonging to the Arab nation, among the immigrant Jews in Israel, and something similar is taking place among the inhabitants of multi-lingual Switzerland.

Summarizing, a distinct language is an extremely important, but neither a sufficient nor an absolutely essential mark of an ethnic group and of its politically significant variant—the nationality. *Mores*, religion, race, tradition, prevailing aspirations and values enter the picture and substantially modify it.

In the context of politics no special importance need be attributed to that form of linguistic pluralism, or polylinguism, which is occasionally manifested by States with a single official language[1] when they silently tolerate the use of other languages or even themselves use them within the territory as a matter of pragmatic convenience. Such practices are quite wide-spread in many a developed country secure in the knowledge of its relative ethnic homogeneity or of the strength of the integration process which is going on in it. Here the maxim of *de minimis* truly applies. What we mean is not only the use of foreign or minority languages for public events of an artistic, cultural or scientific nature, or the appearance in them of books and periodicals; for these things are

1. Only relatively new States, conscious of the struggle that led to their independence and of the national connotations of that struggle, take the trouble of expressly stating in their constitutions that such and such is or are their official languages. Older States which have reached statehood before the era of nationalism (Britain, France, Spain) or those whose struggle for independence had no ethnic overtones (United States, Latin American countries) frequently lack any such statement. Nevertheless, a State or official language exists in them as well.

taken almost for granted in modern States. Quite often these languages are used in official documents and by official agencies of the given State for the convenience of those citizens and aliens who are not fully conversant with the State's official language. Even in the network of primary and secondary education which a growing number of States are consciously using as an instrument of civic education, of patriotic indoctrination and of ethnic integration, foreign- and minority-language schools of a private character are allowed to exist along with other kinds of private—especially religious—schools.[1] Even in the countries of Eastern Europe, particularly sensitive of any kind of foreign influence, such schools are in existence over and above the schools destined to fill the needs of their minority nationalities, though attendance in them is restricted for all practical purposes to children of foreign residents. In other countries citizens, too, are allowed to attend them. In developing countries, more particularly, the use of schools with a foreign language of instruction and often under foreign direction is especially wide-spread and includes forms such as missionary schools, *Alliance Française* schools and American colleges, though local authorities and local opinion often resent them. Since none of these has proved to be an effective instrument of furthering long-range ethnic pluralism, none of them is of major relevance to the State-nation problem, and they are mentioned here for the sake of completeness only.

Of far greater significance to our subject are the demands frequently made on behalf of non-dominant ethnic groups, and quite often conceded by the State authorities, to have their languages accorded an official status. When this is so the least form of such recognition is represented by a provision in the law of the land, sometimes also in an international agreement, granting the use of the language in question as a matter of right in public life, including its use by and in proceedings before official agencies, such as courts of law, parliamentary

1. It is more difficult to grasp this situation in England where the name of 'public' schools is conventionally given to some, though not all, of those schools which in effect are private schools.

and self-government assemblies, and central and local administrative bodies. A typical instance of this kind was the regime of the 'protection of minorities', current in East-Central Europe after World War I, a system anchored in the internal law of the countries involved and partly stipulated in international agreements and placed under the supervision of the League of Nations. In this regime the linguistic rights of the minorities were not the only ones to be protected, but it is characteristic of the importance attached to the linguistic aspect by all concerned that this issue was fought over harder than any other issue involved. As a matter of fact, so great was the value placed at the time and at the place on the right of ethnic groups to preserve and cultivate their group-identities, with the cultivation of their languages as the foremost instrumentality to that effect, that in some cases the right of the group to the official use of its language and to other forms of ethnic self-expression were given greater prominence by the minority groups and figured more prominently in the calculations of the State authorities than even the issue of equal rights and opportunities of the individual in the political and economic spheres. Thus in Rumania, but also in Poland and Latvia, the group-rights of some minorities, especially of Jews, were respected by the authorities at the time to a greater extent than was the equal status of the individuals belonging to those minorities.

Again the most sensitive area in which the question of official status of languages could arise was the area of education and of related media of culture and information; this was so because the media in question, with the innumerable opportunities they afford for acculturation and indoctrination of all kinds, represent an exceedingly powerful instrument of ethnic integration or preservation. Therefore, all forces interested in a specific outcome of these processes naturally concentrate their efforts on the control of this area. Hence a principal demand of ethnic groups intent upon linguistic pluralism is centred on the creation of parallel networks of public schools, theatres and other cultural facilities, in which the language of the given group should predominate and which would be financed out of the public purse on a basis similar to the schools and cultural facilities conducted in the principal language of the country. In modern States publicly supported schools and cultural institutions are regarded as a main vehicle for furthering the population's cohesion and allegiance; hence, where an ethnic group has succeeded in obtaining the State's consent to such arrangements, this very fact indicates so high a degree of political effort and influence of the group that this alone stamps the group in question as a full-fledged nationality. To avoid misunderstandings: it is not, of course, success in respect of a separate public-school system that makes of an ethnic group a nationality, nor does the lack of such a system prove that no nationality is there; but if a network of this kind has been established we need look no further for evidence of nationhood.[1]

Protection of minorities

In the system of minorities protection between the two world wars the international documents of the period very significantly stopped short both of calling the groups 'national minorities' and of extending the rights internationally stipulated to collective rights generally or to separate public schools specifically. The name chosen was the more neutral, the more descriptive and also the broader 'minorities by race, language,

1. The network of separate schools for Negroes such as it still exists and until recently was legally sanctioned in the southern part of the United States of America is not pertinent in this connection. What we discuss here are separate schools and cultural institutions established *in response to the secondary group's desires*, while the example of the separate schools in the United States is one of a separation imposed on a secondary group by the dominant ethnic group. The example illustrates the somewhat oversimplified but still noteworthy distinction between 'minorities by desire' and 'minorities by force' made by Laponce in his recent book on the protection of minorities. What it also illustrates is that the same institution —a separate network of public schools, in this instance—will be regarded under some conditions as a privilege to be fought for (minority schools in Eastern Europe, Turkish schools in Cyprus, Arab schools in Israel, distinct Catholic and Protestant schools in Canada) and under other conditions as an instance of enforced segregation, i.e. of discrimination.

or religion'. The choice of the designation was dictated by the desire to avoid using the terms 'national'and 'nationality' in any other but the State-oriented meaning habitually given to them in the two principal languages of international intercourse—English and French; by the aversion of the strongly integrationist principal Powers of the period—France, Great Britain and the United States of America—to anything smacking of a general recognition of the doctrine of nationalities; and finally by the genuine need to include in the protective system purely religious minorities concerning which no claims of ethnic distinction could be made. Equally characteristic is the *scope* of the rights that were internationally stipulated. They were in the main rights to non-discriminatory treatment of the individual in the political and economic spheres, the right—well established in the West by then—to the free exercise of religion, with but the added step of the right to free use of the minority language, if any. This added step was important enough, but it did not go so far as to oblige the States of the zone to establish special institutions for the cultivation of that language or for otherwise stimulating the group-cohesion and group-awareness of the minority. Individual States in East-Central Europe went much further: it was their internal law that often gave these 'minorities by race, language and religion' the name and status of 'national minorities' in line with the use of the term 'national' throughout the area, and it was their internal law that saddled the State with the obligation to maintain a set of institutions for the positive furtherance of minority cultures.

In practice the attitude of the States in question towards these varying sets of obligations was largely determined by the extent to which the nationalism of the respective dominant nationalities was of a more integrationist or of a more exclusivist character, and this attitude need not have been uniform vis-à-vis all minorities. To illustrate the point, let us take the attitudes of the Rumanian State during the inter-war period towards Hungarians and Jews in Transylvania, or of the Polish State during the same period towards Ukrainians and Jews in Galicia. Where Hungarians and Ukrainians were concerned there was a tendency to be liberal in respect of individual rights but rather parsimonious in respect of opportunities for the cultivation of group-identity, while in the case of the Jews the contrary tendency seemed to prevail. The example just cited gives us an insight into yet another aspect of the problem—namely the possible effect of the treatment of a non-dominant ethnic group on the State's territorial integrity. Indeed, this aspect usually looms foremost in the minds of the State's ruling élite and of the ethnic and social strata closest to it. Where a non-dominant nationality is territorially concentrated in a border region, or where the area inhabited by it lies close to the territory of a foreign State with whose dominant nationality the inhabitants of the area have ethnic links, there are good grounds for our State to fear that any stimulation of the nationality's group-consciousness, such as may be expected to result from a cultivation of its linguistic or other distinctions, will lead only to an increase of sentiments of alienation from our State, to the growth of an irredentist movement, and, ultimately, to secession. European political history offers a number of illustrations of the reality of this danger. The former Balkan possessions of Turkey, the former Italian possessions of Austria, the former Slavic provinces of Austria-Hungary, the non-Russian Western provinces of the former Russian Empire and the Sudeten area in inter-war Czechoslovakia are the outstanding examples of this kind.

In these circumstances the leaders of the State and of its dominant nationality will typically attempt to minimize the non-dominant nationality's group-identification and to lure the latter's members into integration through a rather liberal and egalitarian approach towards individuals. Only where this attempt fails or is inconsistent with prevailing ideas, or when pressured by foreign influence, will the State leaders acquiesce in the granting of such group-rights in the hope that at least this will reconcile the non-dominant nationalities to their retention within the existing framework of the State. On the other hand, where the non-dominant nationality is not concentrated territorially and has no ethnically kindred State across the border or at some distance from it to support its claims, secessionist tendencies are less to fear, and the dominant nationality will both prove more ready to grant group-rights in response to the group's own demands and to assign to the group a special status as a result of discriminatory and exclusivist trends, should such trends exist within the dominant nationality's ranks.

We have dwelt at some length on the poly-lingual features of the regime of minority protection during the inter-war period because of the particularly elaborate manner in which these features were then carried into effect. But formal sanction of poly-linguism in favour of ethnic minorities was by no means confined to that period. In pre-modern times, when ethnic cohesion and integration played a less prominent part in the calculations of politicians than they do since the advent of the twin ideologies of democracy and of nationalism, it used to be taken for granted that where a State had a poly-lingual population, and especially where the several linguistic groups were concentrated each in a different area, ample facilities would be offered for the use of the various languages in official as well as in day-to-day intercourse. Pre-modern States, with few exceptions, were pluralistic in many ways, and certainly as regards ethnic and linguistic pluralism. Integration, with the exception of religious integration, was left more to unorganized social pressures than to deliberate State action. An interesting reversal has occurred in this respect; before the eras of enlightenment, of democracy and of nationalism, the State often pursued a deliberate policy of stimulating religious conformity while remaining fairly detached in face of ethnic diversity; since then, States try, wherever possible, to achieve ethnic integration while tending to accept with equanimity religious diversity. The rationale for this change of trends is not difficult to perceive. At all times leaders of the State endeavour to enlist the moral support of that system of values which is held to constitute the chief legitimation of political rule. When the rulers' claim to power rested mainly on a religious foundation it was religious heterodoxy that presented a potential danger to the State's stability. With the basis of political rule shifting to the wish or consent of the people, the danger to the State's integrity was seen largely in the people's hetero-ethnic composition. It is in these circumstances that protagonists of hetero-ethnic elements will require special and formal guarantees against a policy of forcible integration to which the State might be otherwise driven. The inter-war system of minorities protection was such a system of guarantees. But there were other forms in addition to it. The regime of *capitulations*, instituted in a number of oriental countries over the centuries and extending right into the present century, included as its protégés groups of inhabitants marked by their denominational adherence, by their ethnic type, and by their political allegiance, with the emphasis changing from one type of group to another according to conditions. The provisions for the protection of the status and interests of the Christian and Slav peoples of the Balkans prior to their complete independence from Turkey, and for the status of religious minorities in the same area once independence was achieved, were, in a way, a modified continuation of the capitulations system and a precursor of the regime of minorities protection. In all these cases there was present an element of international law and all of them were influenced by international politics no less than by ideology. As has been noted in Chapter 6 above, international interest in the preservation of national identities and values of minority nationalities has dwindled since World War II once more and is confined today to very special cases, notably that of the status of the Turkish minority in Cyprus. On the whole, the international community, to the extent to which it takes an interest in minority groups at all, restricts this interest today to the rights and opportunities that affect the individual rather than to the status of the group. However, in a number of individual States, as has been mentioned before, formal arrangements continue to function which aim at the preservation of the group-identity of national minorities, with the preservation of poly-linguism as a main feature. The geographical area in which such arrangements principally occur remains in the main, and despite the profound political and social changes it has undergone, the area of East-Central

Europe, with its extensions to the east—i.e. the whole of the Soviet Union—and to the south—i.e. Cyprus and Israel.

The bi- and multi-national State

The preceding pages dealt with linguistic and other forms of ethnic pluralism in situations where one nationality definitely occupies a dominant position in politics and mostly in numbers as well, and the elements of hetero-ethnicity are introduced by the presence in appreciable numbers of non-dominant minority groups. The picture is substantially altered when the State in question is one in which two or more nationalities are sufficiently in balance to present an approximate equilibrium. This does not mean that they must be nearly equal in numbers and influence, or that their respective positions may not shift in time, and therefore the boundary between such a bi-national or multi-national State in the narrow sense and the State in which a dominant nationality faces secondary nationalities is rather blurred. A certain clarification might be achieved if, rather than measuring the quantitative dimensions of numbers or political influence, we were to consider the ideological orientation of the State institutions with reference to the nationalities involved. A bi- or multi-national State in this sense would be one in which prevailing State policy, rather than regarding the State as embodiment of a single nationality, of its culture and inherited values, regards the State's connection with two or more national cultures as equally intimate. Thus viewed, countries as disparate as Great Britain, China, France, Iraq, Italy, Japan are nation-States, as were in the past Russia, Austria, the Ottoman Empire, and this despite the presence in each of them of more or less numerous hetero-national elements not integrated with the respective dominant nationality. Similarly, Cyprus, Finland, Israel, Poland must also be considered essentially nation-States, despite the fact that certain national minorities there enjoy official status and are accorded facilities meant to keep them from losing their identities under the pressure of integrating forces; for the ideological drive that animated the establishment of the State in the first place and that still explains much of its internal and external politics is that of creating optimum conditions for the Cypriote-Greek, Finnish, Jewish, Polish nationalities under congenial political regimes. On the other hand, contemporary Canada and Belgium have become truly bi-national and contemporary Switzerland truly tri-national, in that the State no longer bears a more intimate relationship to one of its principal nationalities, to its aspirations and culture, than to the others. In theory this holds true of the U.S.S.R. and of Yugoslavia, and to the extent to which Russian or Serbian nationalism does not distort the picture, it holds true in these countries in reality as well. A similar situation prevailed also in the Union of South Africa during the decades between 1909 and the accession to power of the Nationalist party in 1948. Under the conditions described there is not one 'dominant' nationality which moulds the State's life, institutions and policies, according to its liking and with occasional concessions to other nationalities, but two or more nationalities which share in this role irrespective of numbers and between which the State is emotionally as well as formally neutral.

A particularly strong indication of the bi- or multi-national character of the State, where the nationalities in question differ in language, is the acceptance or otherwise by the State of the full implications of bi- or multi-linguism. These implications involve more than just the right to use certain other languages in addition to the official one, the duty of public authorities to use them on certain occasions, or even the formal designation of more than one language as the official one. Such a designation, while legally binding, will not necessarily be accepted as conclusive by the observer of the social and political scene. Nor will the existence of public schools in which instruction is conducted in a given language, or the availability of official publications in that language, be a sufficient guide. What is required is that the languages in question be placed, both in fact and in law, on a footing of equality, especially as regards educational and civil service requirements. Here again, Belgium, Canada and Switzerland appear as bi- or tri-lingual countries in the fullest meaning of the term.

As has been seen from the instances cited, a condition of multi-nationality in the narrow sense is marked by a specific state of mind, by the attribution of equivalence to the nationalities in question, and not by a mere institutional framework. The same instances indicate that this state of mind need not be of a particularly long duration, but is subject to change. Further observation will bring to light the fact that the special attitude which the multi-national State exhibits towards the privileged nationalities does not extend towards other nationalities and other groups that may be present on its territory. Towards them it may practise any combination of attitudes encountered before, from individual equality to the extremes of discrimination, from integrationism to facilities for the preservation of group-identity and to exclusivist rejection. Another variant has to do with the significance attached in a given multi-national State to nationality relatively to other social values. Just as it is proper to distinguish a nation-State in which national tensions and nationalism are highly active from one in which these are relaxed and almost dormant, so do these distinctions occur in multi-national States. In Belgium, for instance, the intensity of national feelings is still very strong; in Canada it has become more subdued of late; in Switzerland it is and has been for a long time relatively quiescent. We know already that *intensive* nationalism results from international *tensions*, i.e. from a state of affairs in which the existing social and political set-up causes dissatisfaction to one nationality at least and its attempts to have the set-up changed produces resentment in that other nationality which fears that the change will work to its disadvantage. It follows therefrom that a bi- or multi-national State has a better chance to endure in that form where all component nationalities are reasonably satisfied with the *status quo*. Where this is not the case we return to the circle—some observers might call it the vicious circle—of some nationalities attempting to gain (or regain) a conclusive position of dominance, while the others are driven to the usual forms of protest and disaffection, going as far as secession.

Personal autonomy

Both from a formal and from a substantive point of view, those situations merit to be pointed out in which some at least of the rights accorded to a national group within a State are regulated and administered by representatives, preferably by elected representatives, of that group. Where this is the case we speak of a measure of self-government, or autonomy, of the group in question.[1] Now the usual way of determining the scope of governmental activities in the modern State, including its subdivisions and self-governing units, is by territorial delimitation. Administrative districts of any kind (postal, school, police, military districts, etc.), judicial circuits, electoral constituencies, municipalities, counties, provinces, colonies, bishoprics, States themselves—are all defined with reference to the space within which they are meant to function. When it comes to the autonomous ethnic group, too, it is easy to conceive its pattern if we assume that the group inhabits a closed area and constitutes there the dominant element, usually a numerical majority. In that case the autonomy of the national group blends with the autonomy of the region, leaving as a residue the problem of the status to be accorded to other, non-dominant, ethnic groups within the autonomous region. But in quite a number of the cases noted above the geographical distribution of national groups is such that no demarcation would do justice to the situation. And in other cases, where a given nationality clearly predominates in the State or in any geographical subdivision thereof, the problem

1. Strictly speaking, *self-government* denotes the exercise by a group or by its representatives of governmental functions in all their usual forms, including especially the enactment of legal rules, policy-decisions and administration. *Autonomy* relates more specifically to the enactment of laws by the group itself (or by representatives acting on the group's behalf). In both cases the qualifying adjective 'limited' should be implied, for within the structure of a sovereign State any self-governing or autonomous unit is necessarily limited by the over-all authority of the State.

is precisely one of devising a pattern that would not only assure the group-identities of the secondary nationalities but also enable these nationalities to exercise themselves some kind of control over the arrangements to that end. Clearly, a territorial autonomy would not satisfy these conditions. A pattern that would appear more suitable is that which was developed by two leaders of Austrian social-democracy, Karl Renner and Otto Bauer, at the turn of the century, and which has become known under the name of *personal* or *cultural* autonomy.

The principle as such is anything but new in the technique of government. It was quite common in previous times and civilizations, though not necessarily in its democratic connotations. Essentially its meaning is that the status of a person with reference to law and to political institutions is primarily determined not by the geographical area in which he habitually resides or happens to be located but by some other-than-geographical group with which he is identified. Caste, occupation, status as freeman or slave, estate within the larger circle of freemen, religion, tribal or clan or kinship descent, are the most important groupings which, side by side with his territorial localization, have determined man's standing vis-à-vis law and government. The respective importance of the two conflicting principles—the personal and the territorial—fluctuate with changing conditions. Medieval Europe and traditional India are two prominent examples of situations in which the personal or group-relation principle achieved utmost prominence at the expense of the territorial principle. But even contemporary Western civilization, territorially minded though it is, has not done away altogether with the personal basis of man's status. In the very basic area of citizenship *ius sanguinis* still competes with *ius soli.* The law of family relations is still largely determined in a number of countries by a person's religion. The law governing civil transactions is occasionally influenced by the person's habitual engaging in commercial activities as a means of livelihood. Individuals engaged in particular occupations—soldiers, policemen, civil servants, clergymen, physicians, pharmacists, lawyers, accountants, innkeepers—are subject to special obligations or enjoy special privileges not shared by others. And among those forms of group-relatedness to which the greatest importance is attached in some modern societies, namely in ethnically pluralistic societies, is a person's relation to an *ethnic* group.

Nor is it new that a non-geographical group of human beings subject to a special regime is enabled to exercise some measure of control over certain aspects of that regime—over its detailed regulation and administration—by persons deemed representative of the group. Whenever this happens we have before us examples of personal autonomy on a non-localized basis. Such is the case when a church, a bar council, a medical association, a chamber of commerce, a trade association, a trade union, a political party, a club, a voluntary association of any kind, is allowed to enact rules binding upon its members and to administer its own affairs. And when an ethnic group is allowed in a modern State to exercise a similar role in regulating and administering the institutions devised for the perpetuation of the ethnic group *irrespective of their location within the State* we may speak of the personal autonomy of the ethnic group. Since most of the matters in respect of which the ethnic group will insist on a non-territorial autonomy, and in respect of which the State, when pressed, will be willing to grant such autonomy, will be in the realm of educational and cultural activities, the resulting regime is also often referred to as one of cultural autonomy. It is obvious that attempts to regulate matters such as traffic rules, public security, postal service, administration of criminal justice, commercial policy, taxation in respect of economic activities, labour conditions and public health, on any but a territorial basis would be open to the most serious objections. In any case, an ethnic group that will have achieved the status of a non-territorial self-governing body has certainly exceeded that minimum of political significance which entitles it to be considered a nationality. It is quite in order, therefore, to speak of a national-personal autonomy or of a national-cultural autonomy.

Personal autonomy in relation to ethnic minorities was often exercised in the medieval European city, where limited self-government of various social groups was anyhow the prevailing pattern, and in Europe's oriental extension—the Crusaders' States. Both before and after the Middle Ages it was the regime under which Jews lived frequently in the Orient as well as in the Occident; in their case their double role as ethnic *and* religious group gave a special stimulus to the pattern, though it should be recalled that of the two criteria it was the religious criterion which was decisive: once a Jew changed his religion, the special regime under which Jews lived, including particularly the personal autonomy enjoyed by the Jewish community, no longer applied to him. A regime of religious and ethnic personal autonomy was also widely used in Moslem countries, notably in the Ottoman Empire in the form of the *Millet* system and in the principalities of northern Africa. In all these cases the groups affected were usually, though not always, marked by religious as well as by ethnic distinctiveness, with the former predominating; but enough of the ethnic element figured in the arrangements to make them significant as examples of an ethnic, or national, personal autonomy as well. Quite often a system of closed mono-ethnic or mono-religious neighbourhood quarters evolved, either on the initiative of the minority itself or under pressure of the political authorities, which lent to the personal autonomy a localized and therefore a minute territorial dimension. The European Jewish *ghetto*, the North African *mellah*, the *court* in which German-Hanseatic merchants lived in places like Bruges, London or Novgorod, are among the best-known examples of such localization of the personal autonomy. Nevertheless, in essence the regime remained qualified by the group-identity of those affected, with the territorial aspect playing but an auxiliary part.

Under the regime of minorities protection in East-Central Europe between the two world wars, personal autonomy was tried on a fairly large scale, not as a matter of international obligation, but as a matter of internal arrangements in the States concerned. Traces of the system have survived in that zone, especially in Rumania and Poland, but their scope has been greatly reduced after the Second World War by the generally totalitarian and centralizing tendencies of communist society and by its predilection for solving ethnic problems on a territorial basis. In the case of the Jews of the area, always the most widely dispersed ethnic group and therefore the most appropriate object of personal autonomy, a factor contributing to the diminishing importance of the pattern was the catastrophic reduction in their numbers by the mass extermination practised during the Hitler era and—as far as the areas west of the Soviet Union are concerned—by the subsequent emigration to Israel of most surviviors. Today the outstanding example of personal autonomy of a minority is that of the Turkish minority in Cyprus. While considerable numbers of Cypriote Turks live in mono-ethnic villages and areas, others live in mixed towns and zones, and the essential delimitation of the regime's beneficiaries is by personal, not by local, criteria. Another prominent instance of personal autonomy is Belgium, but in view of the near-equality of the two nationalities in question—the Walloons and Flamands—in numbers and influence it would not be practicable to speak here of a 'minority' problem. Even more than in Cyprus, the mass of each nationality lives in Belgium in fairly homogeneous zones, and for this reason much of the problem is finding a solution on territorial lines; but, once more, there is enough of geographical inter-penetration between the two nationalities to render a personal autonomy pattern a valuable auxiliary means for the shaping of inter-ethnic relations. Similarly, in Canada and in Switzerland, where the primary solution of inter-ethnic tensions between the respective co-dominant nationalities is achieved along federalist, i.e. territorial, lines, one finds the personal autonomy pattern resorted to in localities and zones with mixed populations.

The above instances, culled from the modern world, deal with regimes of personal autonomy which serve as additional means to preserve the group-identity of a nationality whose basic group-rights are acknowledged by the authorities of the State and the essential formal equality of whose members is taken for granted. Not to be confused with this pattern is the kind of 'self-government' granted to an ethnic group of whatever size on the basis of gross individual inequality (Indian reservations in nineteenth-century United States, tribal self-government of non-Europeans in colonial possessions), of almost total denial of accepted elementary standards (natives and other non-Europeans in the Union of South Africa), or as a prelude to extermination (Jewish camps and ghettoes in Nazi-occupied Europe).

Territorial autonomy and federalism

A far simpler situation confronts the multi-national State when its various nationalities, or some of them, are each concentrated territorially to an extent sufficient to satisfy their claims to self-government by setting up corresponding regional units. Whether the leading strata of a dominant nationality and the State authorities are willing to establish such a pattern is a different matter, but if either their own inclination or the pressure of circumstances induces them to do so, the technical task involved is relatively simple. The State itself being a territorial unit, its subdivision into smaller territorial units being an elementary device of government, the granting of limited self-government to territorial subdivisions being a wide-spread technique, nothing is simpler than to take the ethnic composition of the population in consideration as one among several criteria or even as the principal criterion when determining the boundaries of such subdivisions. To admit the relevance of the ethnic criterion in this connection is certainly no less reasonable than to admit the relevance of the size of the area, of its topographical conformation, of past tradition, of the number of the inhabitants, or of economic data.

For various and sound reasons many a modern State prefers a unitary structure in which only local conglomerations —cities, townships, villages—enjoy an appreciable degree of self-government while regional units are set up mainly as a matter of administrative convenience, to facilitate communication between the central authorities, their subordinate officials in the periphery, and the local population. Whatever the composition of the representative bodies established within the framework of the French *département*, the English county, and similar units elsewhere, and whatever the authority accorded to these bodies, their scope of governmental powers is very narrow at best; the principal significance of these units lies in their role as decentralized instrumentalities of the central government. On the other hand, in a number of countries and regimes, important governmental concerns in a given region are entrusted indeed to bodies deemed representative of the population of the region. These, even though exercising their functions within the jurisdiction assigned to them by the central government and under the latter's control, owe their position to their representative character rather than to appointment or delegation of authority by the centre and are presumed to exercise their functions in accordance primarily with the desires of the local population and in their interest. The particular mode in which regional self-government, thus understood, is exercised, varies in many respects, chief among them being the number and importance of matters left to the discretion of the regional bodies, the extent to which this discretion is subject to or freed from directives, approval and control by the centre, and the extent to which the office-holders in question are appointed centrally or selected in accordance with one of the many procedures meant to emphasize their representative quality.

With these variations in mind, a pattern of regional autonomy may be confined to one or a few regions only, or else extend more or less uniformly over the entire expanse of the State. In the former case it is a special regime, an exception to the general pattern of stricter unity. In the latter case regional autonomy becomes a feature typical of the State as a whole. Thus, to go back to pre-1914 Europe, Imperial Russia was governed on the whole as a unitary State, with provinces and districts administered principally on the hierarchical principle by centrally appointed officials and with few and none-too-significant matters assigned to the representative bodies in these subdivisions, the *zemstvos*. Against this background there stood out in contrast those regions which enjoyed considerable autonomy: Finland, with representative agencies selected according to democratic procedures, and the Central Asian principalities—the emirate of Bokhara and the khanate of Khiva—whose autonomy was centred around the persons of autocratic rulers. As we see, autonomy by no means implies that the representative bodies of the autonomous unit must be selected democratically; this latter feature is a requirement of democratic ideology, not of autonomism. The latter requires only that the authorities of the region be *deemed* representative of the region rather than representative of the centre. What procedures must legitimize an authority so as to make it representative is a matter left to the ideas prevailing at the time and place. Another example, perhaps even more telling, is that of India during the last period of British rule. The largest part of the country, known as British India, was ruled as a unitary State by a hierarchy of British-appointed officials with a Governor-General at the head, with the assistance of rudimentary representative institutions on a country-wide and on a provincial basis. These institutions were selected on the basis of a restricted and unequal suffrage, and the scope of their authority was exceedingly narrow. In crass contrast to British India stood the Native States of India with a far wider scope of autonomy, but the representative character of whose rulers was based on traditional criteria of legitimation, without any recourse to formal democratic procedures. On the other hand, in pre-1914 Austria the pattern of regional autonomy with representative institutions recruited on an incomplete democratic basis was generally accepted, and regions like Bosnia-Herzegovina, administered from the centre, formed an exception to the rule.

A further step in the same direction is the system known as federalism. To the formal-minded jurist what transforms a State with a generally applied pattern of regional autonomy into a federal State is the entrenchment of the autonomy in such a manner that the federal authorities may not change the status of the autonomous units, the so-called members of the federation, without a measure of substantial agreement by the latter. This condition is sanctioned by the provision that most of the politically active inhabitants of the autonomous units, or their representatives, or a federal agency so constituted as to represent more particularly the autonomous units, must give their consent to the proposed change by a very substantial majority before the change will come into effect. Hence the increased importance often held in federal States by 'Upper Chambers' supposed to represent the members of the federation; and hence the extreme case of the United States of America where ordinary constitutional changes need confirmation by three-fourths of the States of the Union, while the existence and territory of a State and its equal representation in the Senate may not be affected save by its own consent. From a less formal point of view, a federal State will be one in which the central authorities, however composed, will not make major policy decisions except with due regard to the wishes and interests of the constituent members of the federation. Federation in this latter sense, to borrow an expression of Professor Friedrich, is a process rather than a state of affairs.

A still further stage in the direction of territorial autonomy is the so-called confederation, a political structure described in the older literature as one which holds limited powers by delegation from the constituent States, with the ultimate power of sovereignty retained by the latter. While Switzerland and the Soviet Union still claim to have some attributes of a confederation, the real distribution of power in these countries is such as to deprive this formal assumption of any current significance. Regarding the Soviet Union, it has even been asked whether, in view of the overriding influence of the strongly centralized Communist party, it may be considered a federation at all in any real sense. Similarly, the 'real' and 'personal unions' of pre-World War I monarchies have lost all current importance. Unless international developments lead to the revival of confederations as products of stable inter-State agreements, or a renascence of monarchy should result in new monarchical 'unions', we may leave out these forms of non-unitary States from our consideration.

The reason why these forms of governmental technique are of interest in the present study is that territorial autonomy in general, and federalism more particularly, is occasionally proposed or actually made use of as a means for resolving inter-national conflicts. There were many cases, indeed, in which the division of a State into autonomous regions, each characterized by a distinct ethnic composition of its inhabitants, appeared to the politicians concerned or to foreign observers as the most logical manner of ruling a wide-spread poly-ethnic State. The solution certainly seems plausible when a State with a given dominant nationality conquers or otherwise acquires power over a different people and wishes to enjoy the fruit of its dominion at a minimum of trouble. The way to do so is to administer the territory thus added and its inhabitants in accordance with as much of their inherited traditions, and making as much use of their traditional modes of government, as this is compatible with the fiscal, military and other objectives of the controlling State. This system has indeed been resorted to from time immemorial by conquering tribes and nations. It has been cultivated with modifications, among others, by ancient Persia, by Alexander the Great and the Hellenistic monarchies, and by Rome. It was widely used in the Moslem world and, in the form of feudalism, in medieval Europe. And under the name of 'indirect rule' it was often adopted by the Powers of Europe, especially by Great Britain, in dealing with colonial possessions. In all these cases it was made use of not because of any deliberate policy of safeguarding ethnic distinctions, but because the system recommended itself to the rulers for reasons of simplicity. And obviously it was a system which allowed to reconcile the autonomy of secondary ethnic groups with their unequal treatment, even with the extremes of discrimination. Nevertheless, the outstanding *result* of the system was to help ethnic distinctions to persist and to withstand the forces of integration.

All these aspects present themselves in a different light in the modern world. Where secondary nationalities expect territorial autonomy they do so in the course of a deliberate attempt to secure by this means political and cultural self-expression. Furthermore, autonomy is demanded by them as part of a comprehensive and basically democratic programme, as self-government for the group claimed *in addition* to those civil and political rights of the individual which are enjoyed by members of the dominant nationality. Correspondingly, the State authorities, fully aware of the potential danger which a durably poly-ethnic population presents for the State's integrity and cohesiveness, weigh far more carefully the implications of an ethno-territorial autonomy—a form of autonomy which not only helps to perpetuate ethnic distinctions but provides the ethnic groups with territorial bases and with political nuclei for possible separatist movements. From the point of view of the State, such autonomy is no longer a convenient administrative device; it becomes a major issue and weapon of policy. Nor is modern autonomy compatible in the long run with a status of subjection for the group or of inequality for its individual members—a condition which would have left the dominant nationality at least with the compensations implied in a position of superiority. Attempts of Turkey in the Balkans in the nineteenth and of colonial Powers in the twentieth centuries to satisfy subject peoples by granting them autonomy have failed, even where the autonomy was rather generous and the subjection was reduced to insignificant proportions. On the contrary, where it was desired to maintain a status of inequality, territorial autonomy only gave the subject nationalities a more secure basis in their fight for full equality; and whether on a basis of equality or otherwise, territorial autonomy served, where there was any appreciable movement for secession within the ranks, as a jumping-off point for realizing these aspirations whenever a momentary weakness of the State or the international situation afforded a favourable opportunity. This being the case, territorial autonomy on an ethnic or near-ethnic basis is regarded by most modern countries with suspicion and is accorded only when special circumstances make this concession appear, on balance, to jeopardize the State's integrity less than would its withholding. To a certain extent, though not exclusively, the extreme reluctance with which the central governments of the new States of Congo, Ceylon, Ghana, Indonesia, Sudan, view any developments that might result in an extended territorial autonomy or in federalism, arises precisely from the notable ethnic differences between the inhabitants of different parts of their territories. The short-lived federation of Mali, on the west coast of Africa, illustrates the point very well: begun as a federal State comprising units distinct in their ethnic composition, this very structure, when faced by differing economic interests, by divergencies in socio-political views, by leanings towards rival external factors, and, of course, by rival ambitions among ruling élites, facilitated the break-up of the federation into separate States. In Indonesia the result of this fear of the disrupting influence of federalism was a full reversal of policy: having been established as a federation, the country has reverted to a unitary pattern. Not very different is the case of Pakistan where certain ethnic differences between the eastern and the western parts of the country, reinforced by the factors of non-contiguity and of distance, have made the country's ruling élite hesitate between federalism and a unitary system. On the other hand, Nigeria appears, at the time of writing, to have settled down to an orderly federal existence. While this may be due to a certain extent to the continuing influence of the moderating and relaxed tradition which the country's élite has absorbed under British rule, there are good grounds to believe that this situation has also been caused by the thought that an attempt to unify and centralize the country is more likely to lead to its partition than to increased cohesion. Both factors may also play a part in India which still is ruled on a federal basis. The examples cited here do not prove that the calculation and conclusions of statesmen in choosing between federalism and a unitary form of government in a context of ethnic diversity are necessarily correct: the general fallibility of mankind extends to politicians as well, in respect of the way to treat ethnic groups no less than in other respects.

To turn back to older and more developed States, there are two only in which a federal pattern is maintained throughout with the ethnic composition of the population as the sole criterion of boundary demarcations. These two are the Soviet Union and Yugoslavia. It is remarkable that in both countries the prevailing ideology attaches little intrinsic value to the maintenance of national groups *per se*, and regards the cultivation of national peculiarities rather in the light of a concession to be granted to local sensitivities pending the completion of an economically induced integration process, so as not to disturb the more pressing social changes sought to be accomplished in the meantime. It would seem that experience with past attempts at forcible integration or centralization has also played a part in the adoption and the maintenance of federalism in both countries. In the Soviet Union the ruling élite maintains a vivid memory of the separatist tendencies formerly rampant among the territorially concentrated subject nationalities of Russia and of the corresponding Zionist trend among the territorially dispersed Jewish population. During the period of Russia's weakness, in 1917–20, these trends led, in the case of several territorially concentrated nationalities, to large-scale secessions, and though the leaders of the Revolution did not, as a matter of principle, oppose the right to secession, they certainly were dismayed at the extent of the movement. The fact that, throughout all the changes in the Soviet Union's internal policy, and despite their doubts as to the intrinsic value of nationality within the framework of a socialist society, its leaders never made the slightest move to undermine the Union's formal structure as a federation of national republics and regions, shows the healthy respect in which they hold national sentiment and the measure of caution which they observe towards it. If, during the second critical period of modern Russia, 1941–4, separatist movements among the Soviet Union's secondary nationalities were relatively weak, this may be attributed, beside other causes, to the large measure of satisfaction which national groups, *qua* national groups, had found in the country.[1] At the same time, Soviet leaders were always on the look-out, and continue to be

1. The above does not mean that *in fact* the national republics and regions enjoy in the Soviet Union any more real freedom of choice and of action than does any other group within the highly centralized and regimented Soviet society. Nor do individual citizens in the national republics enjoy any more freedom of self-expression than those in the

so, for symptoms of excessive 'nationalism' among the country's secondary nationalities, i.e. tendencies to cultivate national sentiment beyond the limits set by the Soviet constitution and practice. On the other hand, Great Russian 'nationalism' has been viewed, ever since Lenin's illness and Stalin's removal from his early role as guardian of national minorities to all-Union leadership, with far less suspicion, and this for good reason: obviously, Great Russian nationalism is less of a danger to the country's integrity than would be extreme nationalism of other ethnic groups. 'Nationalism' was also feared by Russia's leaders in the case of territorially dispersed Russian Jews, especially after the failure of the attempts to focus it on an autonomous region within the Soviet Union, because of the implication of national solidarity with Jews in foreign countries and especially, after 1948, with Israel.[1] In the case of Yugoslavia, too, the centrifugal tendencies exhibited by the country's secondary ethnic groups during the period of Serbian hegemony undoubtedly play a part in making its rulers since 1945 adhere scrupulously to a federal pattern. The fact that throughout the Soviet Union's and post-war Yugoslavia's history the ruling élites were largely composed of and even headed by members of non-dominant nationalities (the Croatian Tito, the Georgian Stalin, as well as the plethora of Armenian, Jewish, Ukrainian and other members of the Communist party's top leadership) has also contributed to the result observed. But the decisive factor in both cases is that the countries' rulers estimated, rightly or wrongly, that a federation of autonomous nationalities offers a better guarantee of the population's loyalty than would an attempt to impose a pattern of domination by a principal national group.

Next to be considered are those countries—Canada,

Russian Soviet Republic. But within the context and the framework of Soviet society the territorially concentrated national group enjoys as much autonomy as any, indeed a more substantial autonomy than most other groups.

1. This explanation of the Soviet Union's Jewish policy leaves out of account the possible influence of traditional anti-Jewish (so-called anti-semitic) feelings on the one hand, and of the Soviet Union's wooing of Arab countries on the other.

Switzerland, and lately India—in which federalism is not based *exclusively* on a national criterion, but is used extensively to help in relaxing inter-ethnic tensions. In all three countries the primary reasons for the federal structure are historical, and only one of the units concerned—Ticino—has boundaries roughly corresponding to the boundaries of the ethnic group involved. In other cases, the federated units are either smaller than the area inhabited by a given ethnic group (Canada, Switzerland), or larger than the latter (some of the Indian provinces), or ethnically mixed. Nevertheless, this structure has probably done much to assuage what might have resulted otherwise in very acute inter-ethnic conflicts. As it is, each major nationality or ethnic unit[1] finds adequate satisfaction in being the dominant nationality in one or more autonomous areas. Even the non-congruence between the ethnic and the provincial boundaries, raising as it does problems of its own and transforming the single autonomous province into a poly-ethnic community with all its attendant complications, may contribute in the specific settings discussed to the attenuation of ethnic animosities: were nearly all German-speaking Swiss grouped in one canton and nearly all French-speaking Swiss in another, and were nearly all English-speaking Canadians settled in one province and nearly all French-speaking Canadians in another, this might have driven the country farther on the road to polarization, with fairly dangerous consequences for the over-all unity of the State. A similar danger may face Belgium if it were to progress farther on the way to federalism on an ethnic basis, especially if the present division into several provinces were replaced by a two-fold division into a Flemish and a Walloon area.

1. The German-speaking, French-speaking and Italian-speaking Swiss do not usually refer to themselves as nationalities, and it is true that because their political aspirations have been largely focused on the smaller (except for the Italian-speaking group) areas of individual cantons, these groups have become less politically significant than they might have been otherwise. In India, in common with many other areas in Africa and Asia, the transition from the pre-national ethnic group to the stage of nationality-formation is as yet incomplete and does not warrant the use of the term 'nationality'.

There remains the question whether we can reasonably assess the chances of territorial autonomy or federalism helping to stabilize the political situation and to reconcile several nationalities to existence within a single State as against the danger that the autonomous structures thus established will serve as a prelude to complete separation. Fundamentally we are back at the same basic formula encountered before: the pattern of national-territorial autonomy on a basis of equality is likely to result, in the absence of overwhelming foreign factors to the contrary, in political stability *if* it roughly satisfies the national aspirations current among the groups involved and therefore reduces the tensions among them; it is unlikely to do so if it doesn't satisfy national aspirations and if the inter-ethnic tensions persist. Unless national sentiment among secondary nationalities had reached a fairly high level of consciousness, articulation and intensity there would have been no justification for the maintenance of the pattern in the first place. The solution then would have been an integrationist one if the dominant nationality were liberal-minded; it would have tended towards unequal pluralism if the dominant nationality had been exclusivist-minded; and even if national-territorial autonomy were an inherited feature hallowed by long usage it would gradually recede before the impact of the integration- or supremacy-mindedness of the dominant group. In its modern form, therefore, an equality-oriented national-territorial autonomy or federation is the result of a strongly accentuated demand of secondary nationalities for such a pattern, coupled with the readiness, however induced, of any dominant nationality to accede to this demand. Where the former, having achieved this measure of success, are reasonably satisfied and experience no major exacerbating conflicts among themselves or with the dominant nationality, and where the latter does not give rise to the suspicion that it is trying to reduce the scope of autonomy and to revert to a more unitary pattern, the chances are that, left to themselves, inter-ethnic tensions will relax and the multi-national State will endure on this basis. If, however, this is not the case, even the most generous pattern of territorial autonomy, even the loosest form of federalism, will not materially reduce inter-ethnic tensions within the political structure. This situation is especially likely to occur when there is considerable disagreement between the nationalities concerned regarding the boundaries of their respective domains; when a long record of discrimination on the part of the dominant nationality in the past or its policy at present has implanted in a secondary nationality a deep aversion towards a common political destiny; when the more influential strata within a secondary nationality have become so strongly imbued with the ideology of the 'principle of nationalities' that nothing short of complete national independence will satisfy them; or when powerful foreign factors are interested, for whatever reasons, in stimulating and supporting the separation of a secondary nationality from an existing political framework. In all cases where solutions of nationality problems on the lines of autonomy or federation were suggested or actually tried without success, from the 'personal union' between Sweden and Norway before 1907 to the attempts in Russia and in Austria-Hungary in 1917–18 to bring about a federation of nationalities and to the abortive 'French Community' of the 1950s, one or more of these disturbing factors were present.

Representational devices

The foregoing survey of the forms of pluralism embraces those substantive positions which dominant and secondary ethnic groups seek to achieve in a poly-ethnic State. It only remains to mention certain procedural devices by means of which a larger or smaller measure of representation is sought to be given to these groups on various levels. A first level is that of political parties—the principal channel for the representation of various views and interests in the modern State. The problem does not arise in one-party States, but bears study wherever a multi-party structure prevails legally and factually. Where an integrationist trend prevails parties are formed around other than ethnic issues. But in East-Central Europe during the height of nationalist aspirations before and after World War I a great many parties were primarily organized along ethnic lines, and even socialist parties were divided according to nationalities within the same country. In Belgium the ethnic division still forms one of the principal criteria of party-formation. In Canada the major parties, after having been largely mono-ethnic, have tried with fair success to become inter-ethnic. So are the parties in Switzerland. In Lebanon ideological parties indicate a swing from the earlier and still powerful ethnic, religious and clan-oriented groups to a wider basis and appear therefore as an integrationist factor. Even in Israel the Arab minority casts its vote only partly for Arab lists, and votes in considerable numbers for the inter-ethnic Communist party and for several predominantly Jewish parties. Finland seems to be a case in which the Swedish ethnic minority is fairly solidly backing an ethnic party. Ethnic loyalties determine for the time being the party map of Cyprus. South Africa, Kenya, Ceylon, and a number of other new States have ethnic or tribal parties. However, even in those instances where the parties insist on their inter-ethnic character, there is the familiar phenomenon of parties which make a special appeal to a given ethnic group or combination of ethnic groups and through which these groups have attempted to gain the objectives they had in mind. This process has been carefully studied in the United States of America with reference to the position of the Republican party among Negroes from the Civil War down to the New Deal and with reference to the position of the Democratic party among several groups of European immigrants up to the post-World War II era. Careful examination will detect similar relationships in other countries as well, albeit on a far smaller scale.

Another device often employed to keep ethnic and other heterogeneous elements satisfied within the framework of pluralism or even within a fairly integrated society is the device, already mentioned before, of balancing the ethnic, religious, or 'communal' composition of political, bureaucratic and other élites. The practice is extremely wide-spread and holds sway in conditions as different as those of Switzerland

and the United States. In an openly pluralist regime it is used to supplement the formal recognition of group-rights by satisfying the groups on the score of the factual distributions of positions of influence and prestige. In integrationist countries it is done in order to avoid creating frustrations which might render the not-yet-completely integrated sections sensitivized to a point where undue stress would be laid by them on their group-identities. Ethnic groups merge in this particular respect into the wider category of influence- or pressure-groups, the aspirations of which have to be taken into account by the more formalized channels of government in all regimes. Where political parties are unwilling to be popularly labelled as mono-ethnic in composition and orientation, and would rather gather votes from various elements, they too have to balance the ethnic composition of their lists of candidates for public office. Appointive as well as elective offices are subject to the above rule of caution. Where there is no dearth of trained personnel of varying backgrounds suitable for filling public positions of all kinds the problem of balancing raises no great difficulty as long as it is handled with tact. Sometimes, however, educational and other qualifications are unevenly distributed among the various ethnic and religious groups within a country, and in that case stress on a balanced composition may result in serious deterioration of the quality of the public services. Studies made in the Middle East have drawn attention to this point, and the matter has been investigated more fully in one of the meetings of the *Institut International des Civilizations Différentes*.[1] Nevertheless, so serious is the political need for an ethnic balance that it often outweighs sound administrative considerations.

A more formalized mode of balancing is found occasionally in connection with elective offices, especially with parliamentary representation. It appears in a two-fold form—as communal representation and as proportional representation. Just as federalism is not essentially a device for solving ethnic problems, but has been used in this connection as well, so

1. I.N.C.I.D.I., *Problèmes des cadres dans les pays tropicaux et subtropicaux*, Brussels, 1961.

communal and proportional representation are more general devices capable of application to our problem also. Communal representation is but a specialized form of the curial system that has descended from the ancient world and has been often used in history to ensure a desired, frequently weighted rather than proportionate, share in elective offices to economic or social strata, while proportional representation, in one or another of its many varieties, is a system worked out in the nineteenth century in an attempt to overcome certain shortcomings of the majority system. Applied to poly-ethnic and related multi-religious situations, the curial system became a method to ensure a predetermined share in the representative body to a given group or community. It was first used extensively in this way in British colonial practice and became known by the name the British gave it—communal representation. The system can be employed either to guarantee a minority group against being swamped by the majority altogether, and thus being denied adequate representation, or in order to give such a minority a guaranteed over-representation. Judgement on the device will often vary according to the purpose intended by the authorities which have instituted it and according to the observers' attitude towards that purpose. When used by colonial regimes the device has given rise to the suspicion that it was intended to further divide existing communities and to prevent their presenting a united political front against the colonial Power. It is noteworthy, however, that at least two newly independent States, Lebanon and Cyprus, have found it advisable to retain the curial system precisely in order to maintain peace between groups, and traces of the system are observable in India and a few other newly independent States in Asia and Africa as well. While it is true, therefore, that the curial representation system, as applied to poly-ethnic countries, is an instrument of pluralism and not of integration and that it easily lends itself to discriminatory use, it should also be acknowledged that in certain circumstances the system may simply be adopted for the sake of civic peace.

The one objection of principle that might be opposed even

to the most fairly designed system of communal representation (and to every other form of curial representation, for that matter) is that the primary group-identity of the voter is determined not by the voter himself but by the constituent or legislative authority. Let us take the case of a voter who is at one and the same time A by occupation, B by nationality or language, C by religion, and D by his general social and political outlook. In the curial system it is not he who freely determines with what group to associate for voting purposes. His association will be predetermined for him by others, thereby contributing to the political immobility of the individual, reducing his essential 'self-determination' and manipulating certain divisions within the population so as to reduce their mobility and to give them a caste-like character. The proportional representation system, whose applicability transcends by far poly-ethnic countries and whose merits and shortcomings are well known to political scientists, is at any rate free from this one objection. It affords members of an ethnic group untrammelled opportunities to associate themselves for voting purposes on an ethnic basis, *should they so desire*, but does not oblige them to do so, and leaves them free to disregard ethnic bonds in favour of other allegiances or interests, should these rank higher in their scale of preferences. Indeed, in the poly-ethnic countries of East-Central Europe between the two world wars, where regard for ethnic particularities was combined with social mobility and with fair development of individual rights, proportional representation was very much *en vogue*.

9
Secession

WHEN tensions are engendered within a State between the State's dominating nationality or combination of nationalities and a given territorially concentrated national group this tension ends at times by the State having to give up this part of its territory. When this is done by means of a formal agreement surrendering the area to another State the act involved is technically known as *cession*. A cession, or agreed surrender of a portion of territory, is far from limited to conflicts of an ethnic character. Far more frequently it occurs in the ordinary course of international relations as an aftermath of wars, of economic and of power rivalry, or as an incident of diplomatic and (earlier) dynastic accommodations. An ethnic link between the State gaining the area and the area's population will, in such cases, serve as a welcome added justification for the act of cession, but will hardly constitute its outstanding reason. What concerns us more directly is an alienation of part of a State's territory which, however much stimulated by foreign and international factors, is definitely based on a strong and articulate desire among the area's inhabitants for their alienation from the State in question. Even in this case the result may be their incorporation, and that of the area involved, in another already existing State by agreement with their former State, and this again will constitute a cession. But from the viewpoint of the local adherents of such alienation the significant feature in the process, no less than in the setting up of a new State, will lie precisely in their own attitude of self-alienation, technically known as *secession*. When a poly-ethnic State neither succeeds in neutralizing the political urges of its several ethnic groups through integration nor adjusts itself to their continued existence by dint of a mutually acceptable pluralist solution, such a secessionist movement often makes itself felt among one or more of its territorially concentrated secondary nationalities. Assuming that the movement waxes strong enough, that it finds foreign support, and that the State in question is factually or ideologically incapable of resisting the pressure, the end is achieved and secession becomes an accomplished fact. All new States formed since the beginning of the nineteenth century, with but few exceptions,[1] are the products of such a secessionist movement, and in most of the cases the ethnic element played a dominant part in the process.

Turning more especially to the ethnically motivated instances of secession, we can by and large distinguish among them two types of cases. In one type a secondary national group, dissatisfied with its position within the State, is conscious of the existence of a foreign, usually neighbouring, State, the dominant nationality of which it regards as identical or near-identical. In such a case, our secondary nationality will begin considering itself as a mere splinter-group of that nationality, and the adherents of the secessionist movement, rather than aim at the establishment of an independent State, will aspire

1. Such exceptions were the now extinct 'Congo State' of 1885 and Manchukuo of 1932. The element of self-alienation was originally negligible in Albania, Iraq and Jordan, however much a sentiment of self-identification with the respective States may have progressed later. Liberia, having been established on a different basis, may not be cited in the present connection; it arose out of an act of self-alienation of a group of people but was accompanied by their migration to a new habitat (albeit claimed on historical grounds) rather than by a claim of a new political status for their habitat at the time. This is also true of the earlier phases of the Zionist movement which, at a later period, led to the formation of the State of Israel.

Another group of States is constituted by those in the formation of which the ethnic moment, though decisive, took the form of coalescence rather than of secession—Germany between 1848 and 1945—or in which the elements of coalescence and secession were simultaneously present—Italy, Poland, Yugoslavia. Earlier processes of the same kind led to the unification of England, Christian Spain, France and Russia in the Middle Ages.

at their personal and territorial incorporation (or re-incorporation) with the ethnically kindred State. Taking their name from the movement, which developed in the nineteenth century, to incorporate into the Italian State the 'non-redeemed' parts of Italy, the *Italia irredenta*, then mainly under Austrian rule, aspirations of this kind have become known as *irredentist*. It goes without saying that the State which would stand to gain an accretion of a kindred population and of territory by the success of an irredentist movement is just as keen on achieving this result as is the population concerned, if not keener still. Circumstances will determine whether irredentism is stronger in the area to be redeemed or in the State which wishes to incorporate the area; whether the movement will start on one or the other side of the border or on both sides simultaneously; whether the main stimulus for the movement and the principal causes for its success, if it is to succeed, are provided by the State which appears in the role of the prospective beneficiary or by the inhabitants of the area to be redeemed. In any case, an irredentist movement in the strict sense of the word seeks justification mainly in the ethnic composition of the inhabitants of the area in question.

It will be useful to look at the principal instances in which irredentism in this sense has succeeded to gain its original objectives, has led to modified success, or is still an active force in inter-State and intra-State relations. Among the principal successes of irredentism we may mention the union of the Austrian-held portions of Italian-inhabited territories with the Italian State—a process begun in 1859 and completed in 1918; the reunion of Alsace-Lorraine with France in 1918; the union of the areas inhabited predominantly by Rumanian and South Slavic groups and held by Austria and Hungary respectively, with Rumania and Serbia in 1918–19; the gradual union of Bulgarian, Greek, Rumanian and Yugoslav-inhabited areas, then under Ottoman rule, with the kindred Balkan States between 1878 and 1913; the (temporary) union of the Sudeten area with Germany in 1938; the union of predominantly Ukrainian, White Russian and Lithuanian areas, then under Polish rule, with the respective States, in 1939 and after;

the union of the French and later of the Portuguese possessions on the Indian coast with India in the 1950s and early 1960s. The process, though known under a modern name, is not really an innovation. It has its antecedents in former times; an outstanding example is the centuries-long process of union or reunion of parts of France, long under British rule, with the Kingdom of France, a process not completed until the seventeenth century.

At times, an irredentist movement, though successful in its secessionist aspirations, leads to results other than the expected union with the kindred State. The outstanding example is Cyprus, where the *enosis* movement seeking union with Greece has led, under the pressure of diverse foreign factors, to independence. At the time of writing, other irredentist movements of varying degrees of strength are found in the largely German-inhabited *Alto Adige* (South Tirol) in Italy, in the predominantly Arab-inhabited areas along some of the borders of Israel, and in Kashmir on the Pakistani border of India.

A form of irredentist secession which has been tried out in three significant modern cases is that commonly referred to as partition. We speak of the partition of a State or a political unit when the alienation of its territory in the interest of more than one beneficiary has been either complete or has been carried out on so large a scale, affecting so much of the territory and population, that one is no longer justified in regarding the operation as a merely peripheral phenomenon which leaves the structure in question substantially surviving with only some of its outlying possessions amputated. In partition the amputation has been either complete or so extensive that neither of the now separate parts can be said to represent continuity with the former State or political unit. Obviously the designation is a mere rough effort to describe a very extensive alienation of territory and is incapable of exact definition; opinions may differ, therefore, on the point whether a given process of alienation merits or not the name of partition.

Like some of the other patterns explored here, partition,

too, is far from being a solution restricted to inter-ethnic conflicts. In the partition of Poland in the second half of the eighteenth century we encounter it as a device of power politics bent on aggrandizement, though in respect of some parts of south-eastern Poland that fell to Russia there was an ethno-religious link to the annexing country, even if this was not particularly stressed at the time. This was also, in the main, the nature of the partition of Poland in 1939, though here the ethnic moment was very much alive in the consciousness of the parties concerned with respect to the eastern part to the country which fell to the Soviet Union. Both ethnic and power-politics considerations characterized the partition of Czechoslovakia in 1938–9 between Germany, Hungary and Poland, with first a rump-structure of a federalized State and then two distinct entities—a nominally independent Slovakia and a 'protectorate of Bohemia and Moravia'—left in the centre. Partitions of a new kind, caused by a combination of power politics and ideological divergencies, but by no ethnic considerations whatsoever, are those of Korea in 1948, of Germany in 1949 and of Vietnam in 1954. The three clear cases in which partition was adopted hitherto as a solution along ethnic or ethno-religious lines were those of Ireland in 1921, of India in 1947 and of Palestine in 1948. In addition, the division of the Austro-Hungarian Empire in 1918, in which the distinct States of Austria and of Hungary survived as only two, and by no means largest, among several successor States, comes very near to an ethnically motivated partition process. So does the gradual division of the Ottoman Empire, a process that extended over two centuries. In all these cases the ethnic tensions played a significant part in the process but were by no means the only or necessarily the decisive factor in bringing about the final result. With this reservation in mind, we are still entitled to say that just like other, less radical, types of cession and secession on ethnic grounds, partition as a solution of ethnic conflicts indicates that preference is given to the principle of self-determination of national groups over the rival principle of the territorial integrity of an existing State or State-like political structure.

The means by which success has been achieved in irredentist movements have been just as different as were the varieties of these movements. While in most cases it took military action from outside the disputed area to bring about its 'redemption', there are cases on record where the result was achieved mainly by revolt within the area (Ireland, Israel, Cyprus), by pressure short of force (India), or even by peaceful agreement (Norway, Iceland, Burma, Pondichéry). In every case but those of Norway and Iceland foreign political or ideological pressure contributed to the result. On the other hand, nothing would be further from the truth than the assumption that a genuine ethnically motivated irredentist movement is always bound to succeed. It may be defeated by a show of arms and by an unfavourable international political constellation. Thus the Greek effort in the early twenties to achieve reunion with parts of western Asia Minor, then inhabited by large numbers of Greeks. A number of cases is known where such a movement, fairly strong at one stage, is gradually weakened by integrationist forces sometimes supported by an influx of new inhabitants, thus leading to a gradual change in the ethnic composition of the area's population and in its self-identification. Examples are Savoy and Nizza on the one hand, northern Sleswig on the second, Texas and some other parts of the American south-west on the third. The first was still largely Italian, the second largely Danish, the third largely Mexican in the second third of the last century, and all three formed at the time typically irredentist areas. In all three areas integration with the French, German and American environments proceeded apace, and irredentist sentiment in respect of them receded both in the areas concerned and in the States which have formerly shared them. At times States holding dominion over an actually or potentially irredentist area resort to deliberate policy in order to nip the danger to their integrity. The renewal of the techniques of large-scale expulsion or compulsory transfer of population, already referred to in an earlier context, is a particularly effective means of combating irredentism. It was this method which was used precisely to that end in the reciprocal Bulgarian-Turkish and Greek-Turkish arrangements, by Czechoslovakia in the Sudeten area, and by Poland and Russia in the areas taken from Germany after the Second World War. As a result of such methods, however humanely or brutally employed, an area rapidly loses its ethnic profile, and the continuum of the ethno-geographic unit is destroyed.

In a wider sense we encounter movements, also referred to as irredentist, in which the justification for the change sought does not lie in the present ethnic make-up of the area's population but rather in historical links and associations. The bearers of the irredentist idea in such a case are not found, in the main, among the inhabitants of the area, but among the rulers or inhabitants of the interested 'foreign' State. One form of this kind of irredentism is that in which the reminiscences of an ethnic group dominant in the State merge with the claims raised on behalf of the State and jointly press for the re-acquisition of the area which at some time in the past had been both inhabited by the same ethnic group and incorporated in that State. A modern example is the irredentist movement in Western Germany in respect of lands east of the Oder-Neisse line which were, within living memory, both German-inhabited and politically part of Germany. Nationalism and patriotism both contribute in this case to the strength of the irredentist movement. A second main form is that in which a movement arises within a State seeking to incorporate an area that can be claimed either on the ground that it has been politically under the State's sway at one time or another or on the ground that it was ethnically related in the past. The voices which claimed at different times the 'Rhine frontier' for France, the 'frontiers of the Holy Roman Empire' for Germany, the 'lands of St Stephen's Crown' for Hungary, the borders 'from sea to sea' (meaning from the Baltic to the Black Sea) for Poland, the claims which—for all their Marxist superstructure and rationalization—were silently retained in the Soviet Union between the two world wars to bring back into the fold areas held by Russia prior to 1914, the claims made at one time for a 'Greater Bulgaria' and 'Greater Greece' and, throughout the fascist regime, for an Italy entitled to the lands of the Roman

Empire of old, the claims made in Egypt on Sudan, in Morocco on Mauretania, in Syria and Iraq on neighbouring territories, in Israel on Greater Palestine and in Arab countries on Israel, are all instances of this kind. Here, irredentism is a form of limited expansionism entertained by more or less influential strata within the given State, and the search for 'historic frontiers' belongs in a category not very much removed from that for 'strategic frontiers' or 'economically viable frontiers', indeed at times merging with them. No generalization can be made regarding the validity or invalidity, the chances of success as against the risks of failure, of such claims as against the strict preservation of the political *status quo* of the moment, that would apply indistinctively to all cases. A third and rather exceptional kind of historic irredentism is that in which an ethnically motivated movement for statehood arises within an ethnic group in respect of an area in which, as yet, there is no appreciable corresponding movement and which may even be inhabited at the moment by a rather differently composed population. Such was the movement which, starting in the United States, resulted in the establishment of Liberia, and such were the beginnings of Zionism which, starting in Europe, resulted in the establishment of Israel. Not for nothing have both processes been likened to colonization processes. The element of a colonization of a territory initially apart and distant from that inhabited by the participants in the movement was indeed present in both cases. What distinguishes the Liberian and the Zionist movements from typical mass-colonization movements such as have taken place in the Americas, in Australia, in New Zealand, in Siberia is precisely the element of historic connection and of the claim of redemption based on it.

While secession in an irredentist context is a phenomenon largely connected with an ethnic splinter-group and usually results, in case of success, in union or reunion with an already existing kindred State, we must still consider those forms of secession in which the groups concerned become the dominant nationalities of a State to be newly established. Some of these cases have been encountered already. The Polish Republic which has emerged in 1919 from the convergence of irredentist movements in Polish-inhabited areas of three distinct States is one example. A Cyprus which had sought union with Greece and has somehow graduated into independence is another one. Some partitions have also led to this result. But the principal type of a secessionist movement which leads to independence is that which has deliberately set out to exchange the condition of the group from one of a politically subject nationality to one of a dominant nationality in a State yet to be formed. Thus formulated, the movement has received in the nineteenth century the accolade of 'the principle of nationalities'. Early in the twentieth century a similar purpose was justified by the then current 'doctrine of national self-determination', a doctrine which, though admitting and perhaps even welcoming cases in which subject nationalities limit themselves to a more modest aim, acknowledges as a matter of principle the moral claim of any nationality to complete independence, should its spokesman insist on it. In recent decades the movement is more frequently referred to as 'national liberation movement'.

All these formulations merely proclaim as an express value-judgement what prior to the nineteenth century had been a matter of historical experience, namely that a nationality may tend towards statehood. But the innovation is not without significance. What had earlier been a not-infrequent occurrence, explained as such after the event, has now become, in the minds of the growing number of adherents of these theories, the statement of a claim accepted as morally valid even before the event. Prior to the second decade of the nineteenth century, nationalities sometimes happened to become States. Thereafter the very formation of States became overwhelmingly a function of the conscious movement of nationalism and, whatever the other causes which contributed to their establishment, was overwhelmingly justified on the ground of conformity with the idea of nationalism. In this sense nationalism has added a new dimension to the phenomenon of State formation.

We have seen that the States of America, except for those formed in the Caribbean zone after the Second World War in the wake of the de-colonization movement, do not owe their existence to ethnically motivated secessions. Neither the evolution of Canada as a whole towards independence nor the revolutionary upheavals which have transformed practically the entire remainder of the New World into independent States were due to the impulse of an ethnic group to shake off the rule of a different nationality. The impulses were rather those of a liberally or democratically oriented society seeking relief from stringent authoritarian rule, and the movement's bearers were united by geography, not by ethnic bonds. Nationalities may *result* from the establishment of these States; nationalities did not *cause* these States to come into being. But except for these and for the few other exceptions noted before, located elsewhere, the category of States formed by an ethnically motivated secessionist drive include practically all the States of Europe established at any time during the nineteenth and the twentieth centuries, all the States which finally arose on the territory of the former Ottoman Empire, and—in a certain sense—all the 'new' countries which emerged from the de-colonization process in Africa, in Asia and in the Caribbean.

The above does not imply that the States of this type are necessarily mono-ethnic or at least uni-national. From Finland to the Congo and from the Philippines to Morocco cases abound in which these national States (or nation-States) are poly-ethnic and multi-national and face the very problems with which we deal throughout this study. Integrationism and pluralism, dominant nationality nationalism of the exclusivist and of the egalitarian types, secondary nationalities nationalism of a limited and of a secessionist kind—all of these may, depending on circumstances, develop in the new States which have been born under the impulse of nationalism as strongly as in older States which grew up in a different atmosphere, and, indeed, even more strongly. What characterizes the States deliberately formed under the impact of the doctrine of nationalities is that they are the product of an explosion in the course of which a formerly non-dominant ethnic group or combination of ethnic groups deliberately tore asunder an existing political structure and made itself the dominant ethnic group or combination of a new political structure. Except for the manner of their formation and, of course, for the contents and complexity of their culture, the 'new' nation-States formed under the impulse of the doctrine of nationalities are no different from the older 'historical' States with a dominant nationality. However, the manner of formation, coupled with the State's age, makes quite a difference in the *evaluation* of the phenomenon in the eyes of outside observers. Age and habit, in this as in other respects, serve as great legitimizers. A State that has existed for a long time tends to be accepted as legitimate by other States as well as by sophisticated and unsophisticated observers alike, just for this reason and without reference to its material and spiritual civilization or to the composition or standards of its population. Time there was when such differences were considered of significance by the rulers and scholars of Christian Europe, and pagan or even Moslem States were regarded as of questionable legitimacy irrespective of age and strength. But ethnic cohesion or absence thereof were not so regarded. A high degree of ethnic cohesion contributed in fact to the formation or the inner strength of a State, and absence thereof made for greater insecurity of its position; but neither was regarded as criterion for asserting or denying a State's legitimacy.

With the emergence of the age of nationalism this has changed. We have now a sharp division between two camps. In one camp are the 'historicists', to whom any State which can boast of long existence is legitimate just because of this. Uni-national France, almost uni-national Great Britain, the multi-national formations of pre-war Austria and Turkey, of Switzerland and of the British Empire, the not yet nationally crystallized United States of America and the binational Canada are equally legitimate; but any attempt to change the *status quo* at the expense of existing States on ethnic grounds is considered illegitimate. It is interesting that the same hostility is not observed in this camp towards changes on other than ethnic grounds: dynastic, strategic, economic criteria for a change in the *status quo* are admitted; for all of these, in a way, serve the State idea and are undertaken in the exercise of traditional State functions. But where the impulse for the change originated in the doctrine of nationalities it is an emanation of a rival to the State idea and has to be combated. On the other side of the fence stand the protagonists of the national idea. To them the criterion of a State's legitimacy lies in its conformity or otherwise to the doctrine of nationalities. A State that more or less conforms to the doctrine is legitimate; one that doesn't so conform is contested; and the very movement to change the *status quo* by an ethnically motivated secession movement is legitimate as well.

This, of course, is merely a grossly simplified schematic view. In fact, attitudes are modified by exigencies of politics, by interests, by sentiments. The specific case is judged on its own, not by reference to general principles. Thus, to nineteenth-century Britain, the secession of Belgium from Holland and of Greece from Turkey was welcome; that of the Slavic peoples from Turkey of doubtful legitimacy; to Imperial Russia the Belgian secession in 1830 and the Hungarian attempt at secession in 1848 seemed definitely illegitimate; but that of the Southern Slavs praiseworthy in the extreme. Gradually, however, more and more national States emerge by secession. With few exceptions the ones which have already emerged and have gained formal recognition are accepted as normal and legitimate. Those secessionist movements which have not yet achieved success, while welcomed by the protagonists of the doctrine of nationalities to the extent that their own group-interests are not adversely affected, remain suspect in the eyes of the rulers of States, for they threaten the certitude that nothing, save the State's own initiative, will endanger their integrity. But here, again, a reservation is in order: when a particular brand, or a particular instance, of a secessionist movement becomes ideologically irresistible or politically advantageous to support, rulers of a State will not hesitate to admit its legitimacy. In the middle decades of the twentieth century this position of ideological irresistibility and of political advantage has been gained by those secessionist movements which were able to claim parentage with the decolonization process.

10

Nationalism in developing areas

IN THE preceding chapters inter-ethnic tension and its effect on politics were considered on the basis of their appearance throughout the contemporary world, but attention was centred on societies of European civilization, with a developed technology and with mass literacy, in which communication has reached a high level of frequency and in which the hold of traditional primary groups on the individual is at its lowest. It is in this type of society that man's submergence in his immediate local or kinship group has given way to his partial emancipation from it, in which wider and more loosely built ethnic groups have formed and have forced themselves on his attention, groups which either became or sought to become decisive factors in politics. Less prone than are other civilizations to a meek acceptance of whatever *status quo* there happens to exist, a nation nurtured on European civilization clashes with non-congenial State institutions and with foreign States and nations whenever it encounters them and produces that movement of either defensive or aggressive self-assertion known as nationalism. Among countries of non-European civilization, only a few have reached modern history with an even remotely similar pattern of crystallized nationality and of State-nation relations. Of these few the most important are Japan and China, two countries with highly sophisticated civilizations of their own. Japan, in its insularity, has achieved both a high degree of national coalescence and a feudal State organization of a high order of efficiency; at the point when the colonial expansion of European Powers neared its zenith and threatened to engulf Japan as well, the country's leaders, by an unprecedented *tour de force*, rapidly mastered the essentials of Western technological civilization and, with it, the strength needed to resist colonial subjection. China, a nation of gigantic proportions, whose political structure was not quite equal to the task of holding together the vast expanses of the country, was just beginning to get swallowed up in the colonization process when it was saved first by its size and distance, then by the rivalries among the would-be conquerors, then by the slowing momentum of the process and the growing tendency to accept the legitimacy of non-Christian, technologically backward States, and finally by the world-wide counter-offensive of de-colonization. Power rivalry has fortuitously preserved a number of other non-Western States throughout the critical period. Of these, Siam had made considerable progress towards nationhood in the European sense; Afghanistan and the Himalayan mountain States, stopping just this side of colonial subjection, were still largely tribal; Ethiopia, despite its Christianity once almost overrun and once actually conquered, came fairly near the European pattern of a dominant and several secondary ethnic groups; Liberia, saved through an extended period of misrule from becoming a European dependency through American protection at a time when the United States had no expansionist ambitions outside the northern part of its own hemisphere, was as yet far from developing the kind of cohesiveness characteristic of a nation. Then there was Turkey, with a nation at the core of the empire, whose history had been intertwined with that of Europe ever since the country's emergence, and whose technological standards remained closer to those of the European State-system than any other non-Western State of the period (except for modernized Japan); as it is, Turkey was enabled to survive the critical period only through the rivalry of the Powers and at the price of gradually shedding practically every single one of its hetero-ethnic territories.

The rest of the non-European world came in for a longer or briefer period of colonial rule, formal in most cases, semi-formal or informal or diversely disguised in others. In many cases, notably in the Americas and in the Antipodes, a mass influx of European settlers has radically changed the ethnic composition of the population and has introduced standards of civilization substantially equal to that of Europe. With this, either by revolutionary upheavals or by more subtle means of pressure or by gradual evolution, there came to them self-government and a State structure not unlike those practised in various parts of Europe. The politico-ethnic problems of countries of this type were considered in the previous chapters of this volume at one with those of Europe proper. It remains now to take a closer look at the specific conditions under which the State-nation relationship is shaping in those parts of the world which have been subject until recently to colonial rule, are passing through the process of de-colonization, or, emerging through this process, are facing the world as new States. The case of the few non-Western countries which have escaped colonial subjection will be reviewed at the same time.

The colonial and formerly colonial areas in this sense include, as has been pointed out already, territories and populations which, from a legalistic viewpoint, are and were not classified as colonies. Devices such as 'treaties' and 'protectorates' were amply used in this connection until well into the present century; 'mandates' and 'trusteeships' are newer devices; and neither of them change the essential relationship. An attenuated form of colonial rule is the so-called 'indirect rule' in which *most* aspects—though not the most *decisive* aspects—of political power are exercised over the inhabitants by leaders from their own midst and the traditional pattern of society is left largely unperturbed, giving the 'Paramount' Power advantages in the economic and military fields mainly. Even the formerly thriving 'spheres of influence' and their contemporary successors—the 'satellite States'—might be noted in this connection.

Variations in colonial systems that must be mentioned by all means concern the attitudes of the colonialist Powers towards the eventual goals of equality and integration. The Asiatic possessions of Tsarist Russia could be considered colonies without stretching the point too far. But there the general pattern of a pluralism based on domination and inequality was mitigated by the fairly wide opportunities which the natives of those possessions had for integration with such measure of equality as was commensurate with the practices of the Tsarist regime. Still greater were these opportunities for the inhabitants of Tsarist Russia's Western possessions. Among the classical patterns of Western European colonialism one may distinguish between the French-Spanish-Portuguese variety which encouraged to a point the integration of native élites (the *évolués*, to use the French term) and paid for it by equality, and the British variety which discouraged integration and mitigated inequality by pluralist self-rule. A middle position between the two systems was taken by the Dutch colonial empire.

Colonial Powers justified their rule by citing their 'civilizing mission', and—though the manner and especially the extent of that mission were very different from case to case—such a civilizing mission was undoubtedly accomplished. This does not obscure the fact that almost the first effect of that mission was to encourage among the 'civilized' élite resentment and resistance against colonial rule. In recent decades this rule began to weaken all over the world, and the inhabitants began to share in those forms of political power which were formerly exercised by the colonial Power and by its nationals alone. Since the establishment of the League of Nations we witness the added device of limited supervisory authority granted to the international community over the exercise of power in the colonies. At the present state of world history, with colonial rule largely destroyed and its remains visibly shaking, no more need be said about its variations and implications. More relevant are the problems involved in the process of de-colonization and those encountered in the new States which have been or are about to be established as a result of the process.

Essentially, the de-colonization process, as said before, represents the extension of the ethnic self-determination principle to new areas; paradoxically, it is the application of a European idea by non-European peoples, largely at the expense of their European masters. However, it is notable for some features which, while not necessarily absent from the European phase, are particularly pronounced at the present stage. The drive for political status does not come here as a result of the crystallization of national consciousness among a group which objectively has coalesced into ethnic unity. Nor is it an outgrowth of the democratic idea of self-government. Instead, it appears within a framework of a combination of ethnic groups very much different from one another, the unity of which has merely been superimposed by the colonial Power; ethnically, the population artificially linked together as a centrally administered colonial possession may represent several nationalities, linguistic groups, tribes. Indeed, a far closer ethnic affinity may exist between some groups separated by colonial frontiers than among groups on the same side of the frontier. But this fact, contrary to the history of national movements in Europe, plays a negligible role in the political aspirations of the peoples concerned.

Still less pronounced is the element of national consciousness: the near-primitive conditions in which most inhabitants live, especially in near-equatorial Africa and in the Australasian archipelagos, result in so little cross-country intercourse and in so narrow a social and intellectual horizon that the loyalties of the vast majority are concentrated on far more restricted groups—villages, clans, tribes or, at most, on those sharing the same dialect or language. What unites the adherents of the decolonization movement in a particular colonial territory are therefore mainly the fact and the consciousness of the line dividing them from the representatives—whether officials, troops or settlers—of the colonial Power and the latter's allies. The very presence of those representatives, so obviously different in appearance and so radically different in their mode of living, makes the idea of a compromise on the lines of anything less than complete political separation sound most unsatisfactory, and this uncompromising insistence on full independence finds itself very powerfully supported by the existing international situation with its rivalries between Powers and Power-blocs. The more moderate forms of ethnic co-existence, those permitting of a pluralist partnership of various ethnic groups within a single body-politic along federal lines or otherwise, are therefore ruled out as between the colonies and their former rulers. Only the most tenuous connections—such as are offered today by the British Commonwealth—have *perhaps* a chance to hold up in some cases, and this precisely by reason of their tenuousness. Interestingly enough, the above does not necessarily apply to the Caribbean area, where the more benign inter-ethnic climate, similar to that of the surrounding zones of Latin America, permits of a closer and more harmonious relationship between Britain, France and the Netherlands on the one hand and their colonies or former colonies on the other.

Furthermore, because of the far lesser penetration of humanistic and traditionally democratic ideas, the 'self-determination' aspect, as related to the individual member of the group, is less potent than was the case during the initial phase of ethnic independence movements in Europe. In the decolonization process it is the external aspect of freedom from *foreign* rule that is principally emphasized; the internal implication of the freedom from *autocratic* rule, whether foreign or ethnically akin, of the freedom to choose and to change governments, is far less pronounced. For this reason the prevalence of democratic patterns in newly independent colonial areas for any length of time is even more uncertain than their prevalence has proved to be in the States which found independence in Europe and the Americas in the course of the last century and a half. And, indeed, in a number of newly de-colonized countries the institutions of political democracy are tottering within very few years after independence. The obstacles to a prolonged democratic regime, familiar to us from practice and from political theory since ancient Greece, and particularly powerful in societies in which both traditional patterns and a colonial past have accustomed the population to autocratic-oligarchic rule, find in this case a special rationalization: the principal objectives of the politically active strata in the countries concerned, next to independence from other races, are those of economic development and technological advance; democratic practices, with their in-built braking mechanisms against centralized long-term planning and execution, are thought of as hindrances to these objectives. This explains the spread of oligarchic regimes ruling 'for the people', but not based on untrammelled choice and removal 'by the people', marching in the guise of 'guided democracy' and similar slogans.

The new States which emerge from the de-colonization process enter our field of vision in the present context inasmuch as, just because they are *not* the outcome of crystallized ethnic groupings, they confront us for the most part as conglomerations of poly-ethnic populations. They are faced, therefore, with the same question which confronts other poly-ethnic States: how are they going to resolve the tension resulting from incongruity between political and ethnic frontiers? Will they strive for integration on the basis of existing political borders or will they make their peace with pluralistic trends in one of the many forms we have met already, from limited personal-cultural autonomy through federalism and to partition or separation? Again, just as in the case of older States, it should be remembered that not only are the possible solutions many and varied but that the particular circumstances of the individual States offer an extreme variety of combinations and seriously affect the prospects of success of any given solution.

The variable that concerns us most is the appearance in this area of a 'nationalism' which precedes rather than follows the objective crystallization of nations themselves. We have observed the occasional occurrence of a similar phenomenon in other regions, both in Europe and in the Americas. We should now look at it in the different context of the newly de-colonized areas. The picture emerging is, of course, far from uniform. In most parts of Islamic North Africa, as well as of Asia south of the Russian border, the coalescence of local and tribal groups into larger ethnic units resembling the classical nationality pattern has made appreciable progress. A common political and literary heritage of great age and refinement has made of China a social phenomenon which can be classified objectively as a nation by any standards, and this despite the regional distinctions and the fairly primitive means of communication which stood in the way until recently. Moreover, the upper strata of Chinese society, sophisticated as they were by age-old literacy and by rule over an extensive empire involving contacts with the outside world, have been long aware of the unity of the Chinese nation relative to other peoples and have developed a strongly positive attitude towards that nation and its values and symbols. Manchurian incursions notwithstanding (which, *mutatis mutandis*, played in Chinese history a role not dissimilar to that of the Danish and especially the Norman invasion in English history), we find in China a historically developed nation-State no less articulate, and of far more ancient lineage, than the historic nation-States of Europe. Here, too, we enter modern history with nationality and nationalism both present, and with patriotism and nationalism as largely converging and mutually strengthening factors.

Of the marginal areas bordering on China proper, the Manchurian region had been well on its way to integrate with the Chinese nation before the Russian and Japanese attempts, earlier in the century, to foster a sentiment of alienation, and this integration proceeds with increased impetus under present-day circumstances. The inhabitants of Mongolia, on the other hand, were still, a brief generation ago, essentially un-integrated in the Chinese nation, and present political arrangements have only strengthened their apartness. What has been lacking until the last two decades was the consciousness of a common Mongolian nationality, the self-identification of the mass of the population largely stopping at the level of the local and tribal unit; but recent developments are rapidly supplying this missing element, and national self-awareness is on the increase. In the case of Mongolia, therefore, we face a situation where an outside observer would have found a nation, in its similarity-dissimilarity pattern, existing, but where the corresponding national consciousness within the group, as far as recent history is concerned,[1] has developed only belatedly. Less pronounced is both the objective phenomenon of nationality-formation and the subjective nationality-awareness in Tibet. Whether the population of the Tibetan region, the community-consciousness of which, beyond local dimensions, was focused on religious

1. It is not within the scope of this study to enquire whether the element of an all-Mongolian national consciousness was present during the centuries of Mongolian conquests across Asia and Europe.

rather than on ethnic symbols, will develop a nation-mindedness of its own or whether it will integrate with the Chinese or with other nations, is one of the riddles to which present events do not offer sufficient clues. As against this, Korea furnishes us with another example of a genuine nation. Here national awareness has developed earlier than among Mongols in a manner and for reasons similar to the development of nationalism among the 'subject nationalities' of Europe: the expansionist pressure of both China and Japan towards Korea, coming after a period of earlier independence, has produced among the Koreans an intense reaction of the appreciation of their own national distinctiveness. Where Chinese nationalism is similar to the nationalism of a dominant nationality in one of Europe's larger historic nation-States (except for the added complication of the period when China seemed to verge on becoming herself a prey to colonialist expansion, but even this has its counterpart in the history of Europe, notably in that of Russia, France and Italy), Korean nationalism is rather akin to that of a long-oppressed nationality which has recently gained independence anew.[1]

Of the Japanese nation-State not much need be said. A strongly coalesced nation intimately bound with the State, it has presented us with a spectrum of nationalism ranging all the way from reverent furtherance of inherited values to a boundless expansionism equalling the worst excesses of the aggressive nationalisms of Europe and to the genuinely democratic, libertarian and international-minded varieties. A fair measure of national coalescence and consciousness, the latter held down by religion and geography to greater placidity, has developed among the dominant nationalities of the Indo-Chinese peninsula—the Annamites, Cambodians, Laotians, Siamese, Malayans and Burmese. All of these, except the Siamese, went

1. The problems arising out of the present-day division of Korea into two States, however important in themselves, do not concern us directly. This division, just as the divisions of Germany and of Vietnam, is the result of ideological and power-politics factors, not of ethnic forces. Whether, *if* maintained over a long period, they may result in ethnic distinctions, is a doubly hypothetical question to which no answer can be validly given.

through a colonial experience which increased their sensitiveness to hetero-national influences and intensified their nationalism. All of them face, to a varying extent, the problem of their relations with hetero-ethnic elements and with unintegrated tribal and kinship groups in their midst. At the extreme south of the peninsula, in and around Singapore, the intertwining of Malayans, Chinese and Indians, for all the difference in backgrounds and environment, has produced the same result as that characteristic of the poly-ethnic areas of Belgium and East-Central Europe: hand-in-hand with assimilation phenomena, there is an atmosphere of heightened national consciousness and of inter-national tension.

A mixture of ethnic groups and cultures at least as bewildering characterizes the population of the Philippine Islands. But despite the continuing distinctness and mutual antagonism of several tribal, linguistic and religious communities, a Filipino nationality has developed, both under the influence of more advanced (Spanish, American, Japanese) rulers and as a reaction against their rule, as the dominant core of the State. On the other hand, of the entire rest of the island expanse of the Indonesian and South Pacific regions, only the main mass of the Javanese can be said to have coalesced into a nation and to have exhibited inclusive group-attachment on a large scale (furthered by exposure to foreign—Dutch and Japanese—rule) sufficient to result in true nationalism. In the other instances the self-identification of the inhabitants is still focused on small-scale local and tribal communities, while the primitive state of social and technological communication between these communities still makes for their relative mutual isolation; they must be said, therefore, to live still in the pre-nation state.[1] Indonesia is both the most important and the clearest illustration of present developments on this basis. In the interest of the State's

1. A case apart is that of the Hawaiian Islands, the easternmost island group in that part of the world. The very much Westernized mixed population of these islands is rapidly integrating into a single ethnic community in what amounts to a small-scale replica of the American melting-pot. Since the admission of the Hawaiian Islands as the fiftieth State of the United States of America it is extremely doubtful whether this community will develop into a distinct nationality.

cohesion the rulers and the Westernized intelligentzia of Indonesia are trying hard to accomplish a double task: to foster in the huge mass of their population a sentiment of national unity and to strengthen the objective similarities in their ways of life. Since it is easier to influence opinion by modern propaganda media than to change inherited ways of life, there is no wonder that success is achieved more rapidly in respect of the former task. Thus we witness in Indonesia a spread of nationalism before even a nation, in the full sense of the word, has been formed. Nationalism always stimulates the progress of national coalescence, but Indonesia serves as an especially blatant example of nationalism developing before the nation has at all become a social reality. Since some common factor is essential to national consciousness, it is the common dissimilarity with the Western colonial Powers and settlers that is given this role and that is emphasized; thus Indonesian nationalism acquires a strong xenophobic, more particularly an anti-white, racial tinge. This anti-white tendency, and the spread of nationalism among Westernized strata in advance of the full crystallization of the nation, are frequent characteristics in the States and regions now emerging from the traditionally colonial areas of the world.

Turning westward, there is the Indian sub-continent with its multitude of linguistic communities, religious denominations and castes. But the very number of language groups makes them unsuitable to serve each as a basis for a separate national nucleus; the caste is too anachronistic an institution to find pleasure in the eyes of the modernized, Western-influenced nationalist, and, indeed, it clashes with all his democratic and egalitarian notions; long life as a heterogeneous population subject to autocratic political rule (under the Moguls, the larger Indian principalities, the British raj) has reduced the importance of the ethnic factor in the eyes of the inhabitants; and the struggle for bare survival among the poverty-stricken masses, coupled—among Hindus and Buddhists—with the quietist influence of religion, reduces the importance of political and ethno-political matters still further. Finally, when the message of all-Indian nationalism is sounded by a group of Western-educated intellectuals as a basis for their demand for de-colonization and independence, it encounters, in addition to the indifference of locally bound masses, only one major internal obstacle, namely the cleavage along the major religious division into Hindus and Moslems. This leads to the country's partition into the two independent States of India and Pakistan.[1] Within the territory of each State several ethnic and minor religious groups co-exist, some of these so large that, judged by European standards, they could easily form the substance of distinct nationalities. In a few cases—Bengalis, Madrassis, Pathans, Punjabis, Sikhs—rumblings of political movements are heard, calling for autonomy. India, seemingly committed to a federal structure, tends more easily to acquiesce in these demands and to make its peace with ethnic pluralism; Pakistan's rulers are more intent on maintaining a structure that would further ethnic integration into a single Pakistani nation and take a sterner view of demands for autonomy. At any rate, squeezed between the local and kinship self-identification of the overwhelming mass of the population, the linguistic and caste divisions, and the high degree of indifference to politics noted above, both the pre-partition movement of all-Indian nationalism and its successors—Hindu and Pakistani nationalisms—have been distinctly in advance of that objective similarity pattern that would permit us to say that an all-Indian, a Hindu or a Pakistani nation has become an established social fact. Thus we find a picture substantially similar to that of the relation between nationalism and nationality-formation in Indonesia. All-Indian nationalism has succeeded to the extent of de-colonizing the sub-continent from its British rulers; its attempt to forge a nation after the nationalists' dreams has been shattered, for the present at any rate, by partition. The present-day efforts of Indian and Pakistani nationalists to forge nations of their respective populations, aided as they are

1. It is not within the scope of this study to enquire into the merits of the often-discussed question as to the extent to which the demand for Pakistan's separation was abetted by British policy. It would certainly be too extreme a simplification to deny altogether the autochthonous roots of the movement.

by the existence of congenial State structures, may well succeed, assuming they find the means to overcome an exclusively local self-identification on the one and the separatist trends of the major ethnic and language groups on the other hand.

That division into two major groups which, despite other factors, has stimulated the development of two distinct nationalisms in India, has traditionally existed in Ceylon. There, as in most technologically underdeveloped countries, self-identification of the average individual stops at the level of his immediate social group and does not take in wider circles; but the existence of the two great communities of Singhalese and Tamils, at once linguistic, religious and faintly racial, has provided the respective leadership strata with strong bases for stimulating two distinct national sentiments. We may say, therefore, that in Ceylon we have two nationalities on the European model and two corresponding sets of nationalisms. Formerly, the resulting tension was overshadowed to some extent by the common aim of achieving full or partial emancipation from colonial rule. Now, with this aim achieved, the tension between the two nationalities has assumed the character of the major social phenomenon on the Ceylonese scene. The relative smallness of the island and the geographical distribution of the two nationalities make the island's partition most unlikely, and Ceylon seems faced with the choice between a policy of pluralism and one of integration, both, as we know, admitting of several far-reaching variations.

Less definite progress towards nationality-formation has been made in Afghanistan where, despite a fairly long period of united and relatively stabilized statehood, with a common religion as an added cementing factor, the ethnic and linguistic distinctions between the various Persian, Turkish, Mongol and Pathan groups have thus far prevented the rise either of an identifiable Afghan nationality or of an articulate Afghan national consciousness. In terms of our classification, then, the country can best be described as a poly-ethnic State in which fierce local and tribal loyalties reduce the impact of larger ethnic groups and both stand in the way of the inhabitants' inclusive integration. Quite a different picture confronts us in each of the remaining non-Arab countries of Western Asia—Persia, Turkey and Israel. Each of them has hetero-national elements among its inhabitants, but in each of them there exists a well-crystallized dominant nationality which puts these States in the category of nation-States on the European model. This is so despite the fact that two of the three States face specific difficulties of their own: Persia, through the largely local and tribal self-identification of the bulk of its rural population, and Israel through the as yet incomplete integration of its largely immigrant Jewish population with so many cultural backgrounds. Of course, Afghanistan, Persia and Turkey have escaped colonial rule, while Israel, through the efforts of the highly dynamic settlers from Western lands, has rid itself of any traces of that backwardness which is typical of newly de-colonized areas.

The nationality problems of that vast grouping of States ranging from the Persian border to the Atlantic coast of North Africa and from the Turkish frontier and the Mediterranean to Ethiopia and Trans-Saharan Africa, in which Arabic is the predominant language and the consciousness of a common Arab nationality is assiduously propagated, have already been briefly reviewed. The notable ethnic varieties of the populations in question, the still very strong local and tribal self-identification of many elements within the region, and its division into a large number of States—some traditional, others new—make it more realistic to consider that in this case, too, nationalism, as propagated by the educated élite, is in advance of a socially effective common nationality. Moreover, the impetus of this nationalism is again, as in so many other cases, outward-directed, stimulated as it was first by the desire to free the area from European rule and now by common dislike of Israel, and is not free from a xenophobic bias. If maintained at its present peak it's not impossible that the All-Arab nationalist movement may result in the emergence of a common nationality, even overcoming the divisive effect of separate States.

If we turn to the many new States already formed and yet to be formed in the former colonial areas of Trans-Saharan Africa, we find that most of them constitute poly-ethnic structures in which local and kinship attachments are the only ones to affect the bulk of the population and in which inter-ethnic integration processes are still at their very beginning. There is the further complicating factor that in quite a number of instances political frontiers bear no relation to ethnic lines and that ethnic groups' habitats cross State borders. Here, as in Indonesia, in India, in the Arab world, and even more so, nationalism as preached by Westernized élites is very far in advance of any real nationality-formation, and that nationalism has hitherto had very little more of a contents than its anti-colonialist and anti-white contents. To the extent that political independence has been achieved, the now ruling nationalist élites have a choice between various policies: they can try to prolong for as long as possible anti-colonialist slogans, drawing attention to the desirability of liquidating the remaining economic and social privileges of their former rulers within their territories and to the need to eradicate colonialism in other parts of the non-white world; they can try to pursue a strongly integrationist policy within their own borders, leading to genuine nationality-formation on the basis of existing frontiers; they can try to substitute a regional nationalism for the purely State-oriented one—a course that is bound up with attempts to combine the existing States into wider, possibly federal, political structures; and they can acquiesce in the development of a multi-national pluralism within the single State. Furthermore, manifestations of a true ethnically-based nationalism, such as is already appearing in several areas in East Africa (Rwanda, Somalia, Sudan, Zanzibar), may multiply, threatening to change in their wake the character or bounderies of existing States. Combinations of these policies are both possible and actually observable, and in view of the unstable conditions still prevailing throughout the area it is not advisable to ascribe a particular definite tendency to any individual State within the region.

Finally, a word about the still remaining European possessions or newly de-colonized areas in the Caribbean zone. The formerly noted relative freedom from inter-ethnic tension throughout Latin America seems to have percolated into this corner as well. In a few cases, notably those of French possessions, the identification of the local population with France and the French nationality has progressed so far that, distance and differences in racial composition and mode of living notwithstanding, the existing political bonds have a good chance to remain firm. British and Dutch possessions in the area, though emancipated from colonial tutelage, appear to have settled down at the time of writing to a closer and far more harmonious relationship with their former paramount Powers than anything that can be observed in either Africa or Asia.

11

The international perspective

THE significance of foreign stimuli, i.e. those originating from across political boundaries, has been stressed on these pages more than once when discussing the chances of success or failure of nationalist movements. At this point a somewhat closer analysis of this aspect should be attempted. The mistake to be avoided in this connection, as in so many other analyses of social trends, is that of too narrow and consequently one-sided an interpretation.

We have seen earlier that a somewhat simplicist view tended to ascribe to nationalism both an importance and a permanence far exceeding the real dimensions of the phenomenon, almost deifying it as a supreme principle of human history, and that adherents of a second, equally simplicist, view, moved by their intense disapproval of nationalism, were driven to deny altogether its character as a genuine social phenomenon and to present it as an artificial product of a malevolent or misguided propaganda. Now, a third view, also sinning on the side of simplicity, tends to regard the impact of nationalist movements on contemporary society as a function mainly of international, i.e. inter-State, relations, and more especially of the kind of power-politics in which States' rulers are apt to indulge. Here again a factor undoubtedly extant has been magnified out of proportion and, by way of an odd *pars pro toto* reasoning, equated with the whole complicated process. It is true that considerations of international politics generally and of power-politics particularly lead politicians to support at times a given nationalist movement abroad, and at others to oppose it. It is true that such support, when given, is sometimes expressed in forms so extreme as to include the very initiative of the birth of a nationalist movement in the midst of a crystallized or even of a not-yet-crystallized ethnic group, the incitement of such a group to start an insurrection, and the taking of direct military or subversive action to ensure the insurgents' victory. It is further true that such support, or an equally drastic suppressive action taken from across political frontiers for reasons of international politics, can spell the difference between the movement's success and failure. Any conclusions which might be drawn from these observations are bound, however, to prove erroneous unless due weight is given to two further features of the situation.

One feature, supported by any unbiased study of the evidence, is that most nationalist (or national) movements, whether judged by us to be attractive or unattractive, desirable or undesirable, have their birth in a genuine outcropping of sentiment within an already extant ethnic group or combination of ethnic groups, and the attitude, whether positive or negative, assumed towards them by foreign States, even if taken for political reasons and exploited for political purposes, is but a subsequent development. The sentiment itself may be the reflection of similar ideas abroad, and deliberate propaganda may play a decisive role in its spread beyond the circle of the first ideologists of the movement, but neither of these facts nullifies the essential character of nationalism as a movement born within the ranks of the group affected. Even in those few cases where the decisive impulses were deliberately brought about by foreign States a sufficient degree of receptiveness to the idea must be evinced within the group; otherwise the movement remains utterly insignificant.[1]

The second feature concerns the very nature of the motivations behind a State's attitude towards a nationalist movement abroad: not always is this attitude predicated on power-politics only or predominantly. In international politics, just as in internal politics, though perhaps on a smaller scale, fashionable ideologies and currents of opinion operate side by side with

1. A good case in point is the fate of the German attempt, during the First World War, to stimulate Breton and Provençal national movements. It failed utterly for lack of support within these groups.

material and prestige interests, and an ideology or climate of opinion which favours or otherwise nationalism in general or a given brand of nationalism does exercise a very marked influence on State policies. Canning's and Palmerston's and Disraeli's attitudes towards nationalist movements in the Balkans may have been principally motivated by power-politics, but Gladstone's attitude to some extent and Byron's certainly were the result of an ideological current prevailing at the time, and this current exercised a very real influence on official British policy. If the policies of Imperial Russia with reference to the same Balkan problem were influenced by the expansionist aims of the country's statesmen they were no less influenced by the pan-Slavist winds blowing at the time. Italy's *risorgimento* was judged by Austrian statesmen, by Napoleon III and by Bismarck, partly even by Cavour and the court of Piedmont, according to their respective political interests, but for the Carbonari, for Mazzini and for Garibaldi it was a matter of ideology; and in the final balance the latter was no less potent a force. Nearing our own times, the support which the European Allies gave at the end of the First World War to the nationalist aspirations of Austria-Hungary's and Russia's secondary nationalities, when coupled with their refusal to countenance similar aspirations on the part of their own subject populations in the colonies and with the equivocal position they took in respect of territories formerly under Turkish rule, could be attributed in large part to their respective national and imperial interests; but the attitude which post-Imperial Russia, and still more the United States of America, assumed at the time towards the national problem was largely determined by ideological considerations.[1] At the present stage,

1. There were characteristic nuances which distinguished the American from the Russian position in 1917–20. In the United States there was no self-interest of an international nature involved. President Wilson and his advisers accepted the principle of self-determination partly out of intellectual conviction, partly in order to court favour with their own minority groups (Czechs, Poles, Irish, Jews and so forth). This latter consideration could be regarded as flowing from the rulers' self-interest, but it was a self-interest connected with internal rather than with international politics; it was, therefore, in the final analysis, a tribute to the

while de-colonization is undoubtedly furthered by the calculation of major governments to gain an advantage over other States in their rivalry on the international scene, it would be the height of short-sightedness to deny the pressure exercised in the same direction by sentiment and ideology. In short, the support given by States to nationalism outside their own borders is no different than was in the past the support given by them to movements such as Reformation, Counter-Reformation, abolition of slavery and the slave-trade, to the principle of legitimacy in its different (Holy Alliance, Stimson doctrine, Pan-American) versions, to pacifism, to international arbitration, to the upholding of a free (or a communist) society, to free trade, or to the social and economic uplifting of backward regions. In all these respects, States, just as individuals, act from mixed motives; and to acknowledge the part which self-interest plays in the determination of their policies does not mean to close one's eyes to the power exercised by sentimental and ideological motives. Therefore, the foreign and international factors which influence the rise of national movements, the form their demands take, and their chances of success, may only partly be put down as due to power-politics; for another part they must be accounted for as due to ideological motivations not unlike those which influence the rise of the movements within the ethnic groups immediately concerned.[1]

power of nationalist ideas within a society engaged itself in rapid integration. In Russia the leaders of the revolution accepted the self-determination principle as part of their credo, but tried to modify its meaning from secession to autonomy so as to preserve the integrity of the Russian State (except for Poland and Finland which they did not earnestly try to hold). In this respect there was no essential difference between the policies of the Lvov, the Kerensky and the Lenin regimes. Of course, the spreading of the gospel of self-determination into foreign parts was linked by the communist regime from the first with the desire to weaken Russia's ideological and political rivals on the world arena, and here the gospel was preached in its most radical version, advocating secession and independence.

1. This mixed-motivation feature is present, of course, within the ranks of the nationalist movement as well. While the simplicist explanation to which early Marxist authors and some American commentators were prone, and according to which nationalism was at worst a deliberate, at

An issue distinct from the role which international factors play in the rise of nationalism relates to the over-all *effects* which a triumphant nationalism has on international life. In this connection we will do well to consider separately that phase of nationalism which, under the banner of 'self-determination' and 'national liberation', results in the establishment of new and generally smaller national States at the expense of fewer and larger multi-national States, that phase which seeks to unite several ethnically kindred States, thereby reducing their total number, and, finally, that openly aggressive movement which, still in the name of nationalism, seeks fulfilment in the expansion of an already existing State at the expense of other States and nations.

Where nationalism results in the multiplication of sovereignties the question is often asked whether this process does not lead to undesirable 'Balkanization'. This term has come into use in connection with the international conflicts which resulted from the formation of several independent States in the Balkan peninsula. It does not denote the mere establishment of some additional States where only one existed before, but is reserved to those cases where the new States are unable to live in peace, attract international intrigues, and thereby add to the perils and inconveniences of the international community. No one would apply the term, with its accompanying derogatory meaning, to the separation of Belgium from the Netherlands, of Norway from Sweden, of Iceland from Denmark, of the United States and the older Dominions from Great Britain. It was applied for a time to the Balkan

best a not-quite-conscious, by-product of acquisitive, class-motivated or other economic interests, need not be taken seriously, it is true none the less that nationalism may sustain such interests, may be deliberately used to such ends, and may—no less than other ideologies—be made the vehicle of personal and group ambitions. At most, we may deduce from experience that the respective dosage of the two elements will differ in the movement and among its foreign supporters: while within the ranks genuine nationalist ideology may predominate and the political and interest motivations may play a subordinate role, among foreign and international supporters (especially State rulers and active politicians) the roles of the two elements may tend to be reversed.

countries, to the successor States of Austria-Hungary, and may, with perhaps some justification, be applied to some of the new States that have arisen on the ruins of the British, French and Ottoman empires in Africa and Asia. The mere juxtaposition of the two groups of cases, with the addition of the uncertainties still offered by the new States, shows that the condition known as 'Balkanization' is a possible but not a necessary effect of the division of multi-national empires into smaller and more nearly uni-national States. It is a danger against which the international community should be on the look-out when confronted by a multiplication of sovereignties. One may wonder, however, whether contemporary opinion would regard the danger as so serious, so ubiquitous, as to justify turning our backs altogether on the principle of self-determination.

Related to the possible 'Balkanizing' effect which smaller nation-States formed out of larger poly-ethnic empires exercise in their own neighbourhoods is the over-all effect of these States on world peace as compared to the situation that obtained prior to their formation. Here again, no generally valid answer can be given. Where prior conditions were not themselves fairly exasperating it stands to reason that the change would not have occurred, for the cases are relatively rare in modern times when States are created *solely* because of dynastic or diplomatic arrangements or as a result of foreign intrigues. If change there was, the chances are that previous tension was all but intolerable; in this case secession and formation of a new State may even result in pacification. It is a moot point what invites more international tension: the presence of a large poly-ethnic State, handicapped by the lack of cohesion within the population and therefore presenting a tempting and fruitful field for foreign manœuvres—like the Ottoman Empire long described as the 'sick man of Europe' or even like the Habsburg Empire towards the end of its history—or a series of more coherent national States which have arisen in its stead. Nevertheless it must be granted that an increase in the number of independent and presumably weak States does increase the number of possible points of international conflict and that, therefore, a certain negative effect on international stability cannot be gainsaid. The dilemma occurs not only where an empire is challenged in the name of the principle of nationalities, but, more generally, whenever there is a question of keeping a very large political entity, possibly lax and inefficient but still making for over-all stability, going or of replacing it by smaller and more dynamic States. In our case the dilemma is aggravated because the legitimacy of historical continuity is opposed here by the forces of change in the name of a higher legitimacy of principle, and often by recourse to history as well.[1]

Another question asked in the same connection concerns the 'viability' of the many small States that have arisen under the impact of nationality. Viability of States is measured today mainly by reference to economic standards on the one hand and by reference to politico-military standards on the other, with the criterion of technological development serving as a common link in both reference-frames. Sheer size is a useful ingredient of viability under modern conditions, since it is more likely to provide a sufficient basis for an adequate reservoir of manpower, of space, of economic resources, whereas exiguity appears as a serious handicap. Other factors which affect a State's viability are those of physical and human geography and, most importantly, of the State's neighbours. But the raising of the viability issue in the specific context of

1. The question has been formulated here from a general 'world' point of view. The nationality concerned will, of course, frame the question differently and will arrive at a far clearer answer. For the nationality in question the issue is why *it* should pay the price, perhaps the price of its very existence, for the alleviation of tensions among others. This difference in viewpoints occurs among States no less than among nationalities, and the 'world' interest may be cited in favour of as well as against change. The moral basis, such as it was, of Chamberlain's and Daladier's policy during the Godesberg-Munich era was that world peace should not be jeopardized for the sake of Czechoslovakia—an attitude which did not convince the Czechs but to which they, rather unfortunately, submitted. It is a fact of international politics that States expect different standards of sacrifices for the sake of world-wide interests from others than from themselves. A telling example is furnished by comparing the attitude of the United States to the threat of Egypt to British and French interests and to Israel's existence in 1956 with the attitude it has taken when it felt itself threatened by Cuban developments in 1962.

the uni-national as against the multi-national State is rather odd. There is no sound reason why a 'national' or mono-ethnic State should be any less viable than a poly-ethnic one; if anything it would seem to possess an added factor of viability, *viz.* a greater measure of cohesiveness. The doubts concerning such a State's viability have arisen in connection with the disintegration of *larger* poly-ethnic States into *smaller* and more nearly mono-ethnic States, making the latter lose in resources what they gain in cohesion. The problem of viability, therefore, should properly be viewed as function of the State's size, configuration, resources, development, foreign relations and inner cohesiveness. The greater the measure of economic co-ordination between a group of States, and the more peaceful their mutual relations, the lesser the importance of the individual State's size and resources. This goes for the uni-national State as well as for the multi-national State. But, other factors being equal, the inner cohesion resulting from a common ethnic background and from common national consciousness constitutes an added factor of stability and viability.

The complexity of the situation will be noted when we consider the reverse situation, that in which nationalism leads to the decrease rather than to the increase in the number of independent States. In the nineteenth century this process was observed twice, in the unification of Germany and of Italy. In the twentieth century one further step was taken in the same direction, on the occasion of the *Anschluss*, albeit a temporary one, of Austria to Germany. Certain trends observable among Arab States and among some of the new States of Africa point in a similar direction. No doubt that developments of this kind bring in their wake an increased viability of the resulting larger States and contribute to 'de-Balkanization'. But if we turn our attention to the question whether, on balance, they have contributed in the past, or may be expected in the future to contribute, to the cause of world peace, it will be a rash man who will come forth with a decidedly affirmative answer.[1]

1. Possibly the political unification of England, of Christian Spain, of France and of Russia in the Middle Ages poses a similar problem. It would take a trained historian of the period to analyse meaningfully the implica-

This brings us to the crucial point of the effect on international life of nationalism in its frankly expansionist and aggressively exclusivist phases. The nationalism in question is that of a nationality already dominant in a given State which, not content with the position it occupies in the scheme of things, seeks to strengthen its privileges and to gain further advantage at the expense of ethnic groups outside the borders of its State or within these borders. It is important to recall that this phase may occur in an old-established State whose formation antedates the era of nationalism as well as in a newer State, itself a product of this era. No words need be wasted to emphasize the notorious fact that nationalism in this form presents indeed a major threat to international peace and stability, and not even the 'principle of nationalities' may be pleaded in extenuation, since an aggressively exclusivist or expansionist nationalism is an ethno-centric perversion of that principle rather than its application.

Three points, however, should be made in this particular connection. One point is that the birth of a nationalist movement under liberal, humanistic and universalistic auspices, with self-determination as its only goal, does not guarantee that at some future date this movement will not assume an aggressive character. We have seen this occurring in the cases of the German, Italian, Hungarian and Polish national movements, and there is no basis for assuming that the now emerging nations of Africa and Asia are immune to the danger. On the contrary, since these nations start with a smaller burden of liberal and humanistic tradition, the danger of such deterioration is the more real in their cases. A second point is that the international upsets caused by nationalism in its aggressive phase are apt to be far graver than those caused by a nationalism intent solely on autonomy, on independence and on unification. The latter may severely jeopardize the integrity of a State or, in exceptional cases, of a few States at whose

tions of those processes beyond the general characteristic which was given in the earlier chapters of this volume. We prefer, therefore, to confine the present remarks to the few cases of political unification accomplished or suggested in modern times.

expense it seeks to achieve its purpose; the more generally upsetting effects will only come in as an indirect result of the change of the balance of power caused thereby on the international scene. This nationalism's aggressiveness, so to speak, is limited by its very purpose. The former kind of nationalism, on the other hand, directly threatens international security in as wide a radius of action as it can possibly manage. Its aggressiveness is unlimited on principle by anything but its opportunities. The third point is needed to restore some perspective: one should remember, namely, that not all forms of aggression are by-products of nationalism. The great expansionist drives of the past—the colonial expansion of Spain, Portugal, Holland, Britain, France, Belgium, and partly also of Germany, Italy and Japan—were anything but nationalistically motivated. Economic interests, demographic pressures, pride of patriotism, a simple power-impulse, or a combination of these, explain the phenomenon far better. Nor are the modern crusades for ideological spheres of influence, indulged in less or more aggressively by a number of great and secondary Powers in our day, a nationalist phenomenon. In brief, imperialism—this synonym for expansionism of a theoretically unlimited kind—has more than one root and is as likely to arise on the basis of a non-nationalist as of a nationalist ideology. We might even go so far as to find a certain kinship between imperialism and an a-national viewpoint, since the latter sees nothing abnormal in the extension of a State's authority over hetero-ethnic populations. Nationalism, in conclusion, can be and has been a force of great destructive potential, just as other ideologies (religious belief, for instance, or political radicalism) and impulses (the urge for power, for instance, or for possessions, or hunger). And just as in their case, the problem is not how to eradicate this force but how to tame it.

The foregoing survey of State-nations relations in the past, even in the recent past, has been based on the tacit assumption that both the problem and its various solutions remain equally relevant in the world of today and of tomorrow. But this assumption may by no means remain unchallenged. Developments in the realm of international relations, more especially, seem at first sight to cast doubt upon it. It is legitimate to ask ourselves whether the entire complex of politico-ethnic relations is as significant today and—still more importantly—will be as significant in the foreseeable future as it was during the height of the 'principle of nationalities' or the 'national self-determination' ideology. If not we still deal with a problem of considerable academic interest, but this would not be quite the same as if the subject of our enquiry were a major factor in shaping current and future events. A partial answer to this doubt is found in the knowledge that the major current development of de-colonization is inherently an extension of the politico-ethnic tension to the continents of Africa and Asia. But still the doubt persists. It can best be formulated in a threefold manner: on the one hand, it is claimed, modern economic, technological and military conditions make a relatively small State an anachronism. Assuming that a small State can easily have a relatively uni-national basis, the larger the State the less likely it is to have such a basis. Therefore, should not the entire ethnic aspect of the existence of States be valued down? The other doubt, a natural outgrowth of the first, is whether the growing tendency towards the political integration of mankind into super-State formations, whether regional, ideological, restricted or general in purpose, and perhaps even universal in scope, does not gradually reduce the importance of any and all problems connected with the individual State, including the problem of its ethnic composition and policy. And, finally, there is the doubt whether the very phenomenon of a distinct, identifiable ethnic unit, with its specific culture and traditions and with the superstructure of national consciousness, may not give way before the standardizing, integrating influence of modern communications, thus leading to the gradual conversion of ever larger segments of humanity, and finally of all of it, into one composite nation. It will be best to deal with the three questions jointly.

The hopes connected with the integrative tendencies among the States of the world are too obvious to require elaboration. On the other hand, a few words of caution may be in order so as to guard us against illusions. When two groups are developing a clash for whatever reason, forcing them to intensify their contacts is not necessarily the best way to pacify them. It may even intensify the clash. Nor will the prospect of co-existing closely on terms of equality be a guarantee of success: equality will not satisfy those who, either because of beliefs or because of interests, will wish to see themselves, or their ideas, or their way of life, dominant in the combination. When there is no clash and no outstanding issue, close contacts ('rubbing shoulders') may on occasion deepen friendship, encourage mutual understanding, and even bring about full integration; though they may also breed conflicts. When there is mutual recrimination to begin with, closer contacts are more likely to increase irritation, not to decrease it. In these cases the old Yankee proverb will apply: 'Good fences make good neighbours'. Abolishing fences, in such cases, will produce the opposite effect.

A few illustrations will help to clarify the point. An attempt was made to end ethnic clashes in Austria-Hungary by converting it into a federation. It failed. Norwegians at the beginning of the century, Icelanders at a later juncture, had found themselves in a near-federal relation with Swedes and Danes respectively. All those involved were very kindred, very civilized, very moderate peoples. But in both cases the partners who had thought themselves to be at a slight disadvantage in the combination, rather than apply themselves to remove the disadvantage, removed themselves from the combination and chose independence. Now there has developed a truly friendly co-operation among these Scandinavian peoples, but it is a combination predicated on their continued political and ethnic distinctness, without the slightest indication of a desire to renounce either. India—herself a combination of many ethnic groups—constituted under British rule a combined body-politic of which Burma was a part. Now this entity has dissolved (some claim under British stimulus, but the point is that it *stayed* dissolved after the stimulus has disappeared) into three distinct bodies-politic: India, Pakistan and Burma. Only now, after two world wars have burned out (one doesn't know yet how thoroughly) many of Western Europe's national ambitions and enmities, and in the face of pressure by the gigantic forces of the Soviet Union and the United States of America, do the nationalities of Western Europe, as represented by their States, take slow steps in the direction of regional integration. Similar attempts of the Arab States to coalesce through the medium of the Arab League or otherwise, and the much older attempts of Latin American republics, or of some of them, to federate, do not yet allow a definite conclusion as to their ultimate success. In Africa a few attempts of a similar nature have been undertaken, sponsored by differing combinations of States, all with as yet uncertain results, to some extent mutually competitive, and partly moved by a desire to dominate partners rather than to co-operate with them.

It seems that in Europe, where the nations have more or less achieved their political aspirations within the framework of independence or autonomy and the States had ample experience of the dangers as well as of the blessings of sovereignty, both begin to down-grade the values concerned; hence the simultaneous diminution of national tensions and of the fierce competitiveness between States—a process which is going on, for all their difference, in Eastern as well as in Western Europe. The process is very recent, and we may not be certain that it is irreversible. It would be premature, therefore, to draw any conclusions from it. The most we can do is to note that some kind of correlation exists between diminution of national tensions and the greater readiness of the States of the respective area to co-operate. It is advisable to remember that this improved atmosphere has been brought about, despite sharp ideological and power-bloc rivalries, after the ethnic groups concerned have been given ample opportunity for self-determination and the national problem has thus been substantially solved. In the Americas, too, strong forces of inter-State co-operation are at work, and there is a good likelihood of the phenomenon, beside being connected with the economic leadership of the United States and with the circumstances of the cold war, being related to the absence on that continent of strong ethnic tensions (except for the colour problem in the United States). However, in the two continents of Africa and Asia nationalism, whether based on nations already in existence or trying to create them, is celebrating its first triumphs. This writer and his readers will certainly wish the new States of the two continents that they find a way to hold their nationalism to a more peaceful and co-operative mould than did the nations of Europe in the past; but that, at least in those continents, State-nation relations are still a crucial problem for the future, and not a mere academic subject dealing with the past, can hardly be doubted.

It remains to consider the role of inter-State organizations of diverse types—alliances, leagues, commonwealth-type, technical, political, economic or all-purposes unions—whether of a regional or of a universal character, viewed in their purely institutional capacity. It is well to determine what it is that holds such organizations together. If they are cemented by common ideology, by common dangers, or by the unifying pressure of a hegemon Power, this is too precarious a basis for long-term integrative trends. When the unifying tendency is due to the pressure of a hegemon Power, resentments, however suppressed, grow among the non-dominant partners of the combination and may threaten it whenever the international situation should favour such a change. If the combination is based, wholly or in part, on strategic, political or ideological grounds, it is really an alliance or bloc dedicated to the attainment of certain objectives common to its members. Such a combination, however laudable it may appear to its advocates, may appear anything but laudable to those States that have opposite interests or viewpoints, and is subject to so many vicissitudes both of international life and of internal change that its value as a long-term moderator of inter-ethnic political tensions must be seriously doubted. The above does not apply to those well-nigh universal organizations of general scope (League of Nations, United Nations) or of a non-political character (the International Administrative Unions, Unesco and the other Specialized Agencies, the International Court of Justice), nor to those regional organizations devoted to social and cultural ends whose constructive work greatly outweighs any controversial elements in their set-up. The contribution which organizations of this kind can make to the appeasement of inter-ethnic and other tensions is undeniable, but equally undeniable is the fact that the basic tension-causing issues have not been appreciably affected by them.

But let us assume that inter-State co-operation, regional, by ideological groupings, or universal, will further progress. Would that mean that the ethnic and national basis of most States would lose its meaning? This author is rather inclined to take the opposite view. In a world of States which regard themselves as potential if not actual rivals there is a strong incentive for State rulers to seek frontiers calculated to increase its economic viability, to strengthen its defensive potential, to improve its bargaining position. The congruence between the State's territory and a given ethnic group becomes, in the circumstances, only one of several considerations, and by no means the most important one. But within a genuinely peaceful, co-operative community of States—whether partial or world-wide—the importance of strategic borders, of access to the open sea, of the availability of raw materials and of fuel and of ready markets within the territory, is bound to recede. Even economic development and monetary policy tend, in such a community, to be planned and carried out in concert. What, then, remains as a reasonable criterion for the demarcation of boundaries between the individual States within the community? With economic autarchy and military advantage eliminated as major criteria, the demarcation could conceivably proceed (or be justified after the event) on the basis of a somewhat arbitrary division for administrative convenience along the lines of French *départements*; of straight lines drawn on the map, as was done in delineating some of the State boundaries in the Western United States and some colonial boundaries in Africa; of a division of the community into roughly equal portions of population (as in parliamentary constituencies) or territory. The common denominator in these various modes of demarcation is that no consideration is given by any of them to the ethnic composition of the population and to the differences in its ways of life. If mankind were a homogeneous mass starting from scratch this is how it might have been done. But mankind does not start from scratch. Ethnic distinctions which express themselves in cultural diversities do exist. Most States existing today bear each a special relation to a given or developing ethnic group. The average citizen of a State is committed by his awareness of his ethnic bonds in some cases, and by a desire to see such an ethnic link forged in others, no less than he is committed by allegiance to his State. Therefore there is a strong probability that, with the recession of economic and military and Power-politics considerations, the ethnic criterion will gain in significance as a basis for statehood and that the nation-State, rather than becoming an anachronism, will become the rule. The more so since, where economic and military policy will be ever more co-ordinated within a larger inter-State framework, the energies of the State as such are bound to focus increasingly on the cultural domain, i.e. precisely on the domain in which ethnic peculiarities are most directly expressed.

This does not mean that the list of nations and States of the future must be a replica of those familiar to us today. National groups which exist today may disintegrate, amalgamate in new combinations, and new nations may be formed where today we have but an ethnically inchoate mass of humanity. Still less stability will be expected by the present generation, which has witnessed the appearance and disappearance of so many States, in respect of the list of States. The difference will be one of kind as well. Bereft of the *ius belli ac pacis* (the right to choose at will between war and peace), bound to conduct its activities within the binding framework of a wider community or of several interlocking communities, the State here envisaged will have lost the quality long known as sovereignty and will rather become something like a Swiss canton, a Canadian province, a State in the United States, a German or Austrian *Land*, or a republic of the Soviet Union. Many a reader will consider this a change to the good, and this author will certainly agree with them. But it is important to remember that this most optimistic, almost visionary, prospect which may be held out to mankind is only conceivable if the tensions between nations are essentially overcome, and this, in its turn, requires that the relationship between ethnic groups both within the individual State and internationally is put on a basis which will give the groups involved the least ground to feel frustrated. Strange as it may sound, the way to tame the excesses of nations and of sovereign States at one and the same time may be to satisfy the one while limiting the other.

A still further vision may consist in nations themselves disappearing from the earth under the pressure of integrative forces, and ethnic differences giving way to a world-wide conformity of language, *mores* and ethnic group-feeling. The vision may be a pleasing one to some observers, a disturbing one to others. As far as present indications go, it is so remote, so unrealistic, that there is not much point in speculating about it. For the present century, and probably for a good many centuries to come, nations are here to stay. Rather than dream about their disappearance, it is better to learn how to live with them.

Index

(The same entry is used wherever practical for a country and an ethnic group, e.g. Armenia = Armenians, Arabs = Arab countries, China = Chinese, etc.)